Fiji and Me

Fiji and Me

Carol Phillips

To order additional copies of this book, contact:
Xlibris Corporation
1-888-795-4274
www.Xlibris.com
Orders@Xlibris.com

*For my children, Janet, Charles, Nancy and Elizabeth,
and especially for Joan who lived some time with
me in Fiji, and loved it as much as I did.*

CONTENTS

CHAPTER 1

Joining the Peace Corps

THE QUESTION I was often asked was why a fifty-seven-year old woman wanted to join the Peace Corps and go to Fiji for two years. I was head nurse of the Duke Clinic teaching doctors to be family docs. I was working ten hours a day scheduling fifty-four docs. In a brief moment of rest, I thought of the old song, "Is that all there is?" I had always liked to travel. My kids were grown and relatively settled. One night at a party, I sat with an interesting man who turned out to be a Peace Corps recruiter. I asked him about it and said I might be interested. He said, "When can we get together and talk?" So the next day, I began the process and signed up.

About a month later, I received a call which said that I had been accepted, and that there was a place for me in Africa. I asked for more information and was told that there were two seasons, wet and dry, and the roads were impassable in both. The endemic diseases were malaria, yellow fever, and quite a few more lethal diseases. I said that it didn't sound like a match for me, and asked if there was any other place. The person said, "One, but you wouldn't want it, it's Fiji." I said, "I'll take it, do not give it to anyone else, please."

I then dashed down to the library to find out where Fiji was and whatever information I could get. There are three hundred of the Fiji Islands and about one hundred are inhabited. They were once called the "Cannibal Islands" because Europeans, which meant anyone with a white skin, who landed there were indeed killed and eaten. Later, when they began to be welcomed, the Europeans tried to buy land from the Fijians so they could start rice and copra plantations. The Fijians, who knew the land belonged to everyone, had no concept of selling land, but cheerfully took whatever was offered for their land. The planters tried to get the Fijians to work for them, which they would do for a day, for the fun of it. They were definitely not interested in any long-term work. Fijians are wonderful people, but most would much rather sit and talk with you or have a nap than work. Since laborers were needed, people from India were brought over as indentured helpers for five years. The Indians liked Fiji so much that they stayed; and when I was there, the population was about half Fijians and half Indians. There was so much more information and all of it fascinated me.

I was hooked on Fiji and ready for the screening process which was held in D.C. There was quite a group, mostly very young people just out of college. We were told stories of a number of strange things we might expect and encouraged to respond. We were also told that we weren't going into the Peace Corps to save the world, but to share whatever knowledge or skill we had, and then leave. A number of people decided that week that Fiji was not for them. The staff eliminated several. There were about fifty of us left who signed up. We were given a number of "shots" and a room to recover in. Then we were sent home to get our affairs in order, and go to training in Fiji.

I gave Duke a month's notice, rented my house to a nurse friend who wanted it, stored my furniture, and was ready to go. My children were not enthusiastic but supported my decision.

As the time came for me to leave my home in Durham, my daughter, Joan drove with me to Spartanburg, S.C. We were to visit for a couple of days, and leave my car there for daughter, Liz, to drive while I was away..

It was while I was in the shower on the morning I was to leave for Fiji that I decided that the whole idea had been madness. Why would I, at my age, want to go half way around the world to a place I had to look up on the globe to be sure it really existed? I had quit my very responsible and demanding job, but could find another easily. I had rented my house, but the people hadn't moved in yet. I loved and enjoyed my family and friends. Why should I leave them for two years? I went back over my reasons for deciding to go in the first place: (1) For the first time in my life there was no one depending on me; (2) I was tired because my work had been keeping me running for ten hours a day to stay in place; and (3) I liked travel. (4) I liked the idea of helping people to help themselves. But--

As I came into my daughter's kitchen for breakfast, both of my daughters started to ask, "How can we help? What still needs to be done?" "Not a thing," said I, "I've decided not to go." They laughed. My own beloved daughters wouldn't take me seriously --rescue me. It seemed I had to go.

The ride to the airport was full of jokes and admonitions, "Write often. Be careful of those big Fijians. Send lots of pictures." Then I was on the plane, without a tear—wonderful me. As I saw the ground receding, the tears came and went on all the way to Atlanta, my first stop. In the airport lounge, I met another member of our group who was also waiting for the plane to Los Angeles. He looked as forlorn as I felt. As we talked, the sense of adventure and, excitement returned.

At the airport in L.A., with the whole training group reunited, I was happy to see the people I had especially enjoyed during the training. We talked about the things we had done to get ready to go and things we had learned about Fiji. Some new ones to me were that it was about seven hundred miles north of Australia; and that while it was cold November here, it was the beginning of summer there. We were all fascinated by the old name "The Cannibal Islands."

The plane took off at sunset, and as we flew out over the edge of the west coast, I watched the city lights recede behind us. I had a moment of sheer terror before I breathed deeply and knew I was right where I wanted to be—on the way to Fiji.

CHAPTER 2

The Longest Plane Trip Ever

THIS WAS THE longest airplane trip I had ever taken and it seemed even longer when I found that we left on November 29th and arrived in Fiji on December 1st. We had lost a whole day because we crossed the international date line. We arrived at about 3:00A.M, and the first thing I did was to look up at the stars. The constellations were all different and beautiful. I was on the other side of the earth. For some strange and wonderful reason, I felt that this was a new life and I had been born again right here. There was plenty of time to look because the plane was early, and our staff escorts were not there to meet us. I checked out all the new constellations and explored the airport. The customs folk had dealt with Peace Corps people before and as we were allowed only fifty pounds of luggage, they got us through quickly. Our escorts finally came and we boarded a bus to Nadi, the nearest town, from the only place in the Fijis where the big planes could land. It was getting light and there was so much to see. All the plants and trees were unfamiliar and beautiful. I saw a yoke of oxen ploughing a field, grass huts which were homes called *bures*, and all the men were in skirts. I later found out that the "skirts" were called *sulus* and found them quite dashing. Fijian men were tall, handsome, and had great legs. We were taken to a rest house, but were all too excited to rest. As soon as we were given our Fijian "walking about money" which was three dollars a day, we were off to explore. The money is beautiful. It is done in exotic colors and has a picture of Queen Elizabeth on it. However, if you hold it up to the light, you can see an image of the great Chief Cakabau. There was so much to see and do. There were many Indian shops where the shopkeeper came out and urged you to come in and see his wonderful bargains. There were a number of Chinese restaurants. We had been told to return at dinner time to get our supplies which included a mosquito net and linens for our bed. We soon found out how necessary the mosquito net was.

We were given ceremonial welcomes first by an Indian woman. Later, a Fijian man gave us the traditional *yaqona* ceremony. This is very important to the Fijians. *Yaqona* is also called *grog* or *kava*. It is made from the root of a bush which is dried and then pounded to a powder. It is mixed with water in a very traditional way and served in a coconut shell. The person who presents it turns in a circle honoring each direction. After it is handed to the drinker, everyone claps three times. Then it must be drunk all at once and there are three more claps. If this is presented to a visitor in a village, he or she can always come back there to live any time. The effect of the drink is slightly soporific but a lot makes the person very sleepy. In most of the villages, kava is drunk every night. This was helpful information.

Later, we had a Fijian meal of roast pork, *dalo*, a root vegetable, and something green cooked in coconut milk. After dinner, we were given shots for typhoid, tetanus and gamma globulin for hepatitis which is endemic here. We were given that every four months.

The day had seemed to be years long, but I wasn't ready for sleep. I had two roommates who both were sound asleep when I got in from watching the stars. One, named Jane, had been working in the fisheries program in Samoa for two years. She was different in a way I hoped to become.

The next morning, we were loaded onto a bus to go to Suva, the capitol of Fiji. Then followed one of the most eventful rides I've ever had in my life. Van, who was our leader, a very nice funny man, said that part of the road was out. We thought that he meant 100 yards or so, but it turned out to be thirty miles. We were in an open bus, and the window curtains were all pulled down because it was raining. My seatmate was Paul, the man I'd met in Atlanta. He and I laughed all the way. He kept telling me imaginary headlines such as, "Search for the bodies of forty five Peace Corps volunteers continues, " I said, "I'm not going to tell my kids about this or they will insist I come home." The road was up and down mountainsides with the ocean several hundred feet below. This was my first real view of the Pacific Ocean and it was exquisite. The road was unpaved and ungraded and most of it was at a forty five degree angle. The driver was intrepid and forged ahead. There were a lot of one-lane wooden bridges at which you had to wait your turn to cross. At one time, Paul said, "Don't look down because there's nothing there." I did look, and got pretty scared because I could see that we were tilted above the ocean 200 feet below. They don't believe in guard rails. I said, "If we could be guaranteed that we were going to get there, I'd be enjoying every minute." We were sitting toward the back of the bus and Paul was next to the window. He was really muddy; each little hair on his arm was standing up with mud. We had been given a *sulu* a length of material which had many uses. Mine was green with big hibiscus flowers on it. However, it had been packed, so Paul lent me his to wrap up in and get a little less muddy. I put on my sunglasses to keep the mud out of my eyes. We kept laughing. Obviously, we did get there. Ours was such a good group because they made everything fun. I helped because I was really enjoying it.

When we arrived, we were surprised and pleased to see that we were to be quartered in a nice looking, two-story building built into the hillside. There was a real lobby and we found that it was called the "President Hotel." Someone exploring found a hot tub, so a group of us immediately put on bathing suits and got in. I heard, "Don't tell the folks back home that they are putting their taxes into hot tubs for us." I said that I'd much rather put my taxes into those than war.

They soon served dinner which was the best food we had gotten in Fiji. After dinner, the country director came to meet us and introduce the Peace Corps staff. I started to get sleepy, which hadn't happened since I arrived in Fiji a couple of days before. The Fijian nurse gave a long presentation on how to keep healthy. It was all familiar to me and I kept nodding off. We each had to pick a fruit or vegetable and present its benefits to the group. I got a pineapple or *pineappu*. I'm not sure I did it justice. I found out later that they grow almost wild here, and if you just cut off the top, and put it on the ground, a new one will grow. I had my own little pineapple plantation in time and left it for others to enjoy.

Fijian money

CAROL PHILLIPS

Peace Corps in saris at Hindu wedding

FIJI AND ME

CHAPTER 3

Training

AT THIS POINT, we moved to a boarding school which was empty because it was the summer vacation. Our training was rigorous with classes in culture, geography, and more focus on language especially for those who knew they would be sent to a place where that language was the primary one. We were sent to interview various people in Suva who would have an influence on our work. A mild-mannered librarian in our group was kept waiting for a long time by an Indian politician and was accused of being a spy. We found later that there were a number of people who thought we were spies. I was welcomed by a pleasant member of the Ministry of Health.

Those of us in health care were also oriented to the health care institutions: the main hospital which was about fifty years old, the mental hospital, and the leprosy hospital. I first visited the mental hospital. There is one psychiatrist for all the inhabited Fiji Islands. The building is about 100 years old and they separate the patients in something like horse stalls with wooden bars across the doors. The matron, who is the only psychiatric nurse in Fiji, is an amazing woman. She lives on the place and knows everything about what is happening. One of the patients was a giant, over 7 feet tall, who is also diabetic. He was in one of the solitary confinement stalls. I asked why, and she said that he had lost control and started breaking things up in the morning. She looked at him through the bars and asked, "Are you all right now?" He turned his huge head and looked into her eyes. She said, "You are all right now," and let him out. She is totally dedicated to her patients. She knows them and cares about each one. She is a tiny Indian woman and most Fijians are tall and large, but she and three nurses who she has trained keep the place running. They do an amazing job with limited resources.

We lived in the dormitories of the school. The mattress on my bed was made of coconut husks and conformed to the body of whoever had slept in the bed before me. We discovered many geckos, small lizards which live on the walls and ceilings of each room. They are welcome because they eat mosquitos and other unwelcome critters. I got quite fond of them and had several adventures with them. For a while, I had several who kept me company. When I ate a banana, I left little pieces out for them. I found the one who lived under my clock trying to pull a piece of banana under it. They are dear little pets. One day, I felt something fall on the back of my neck. I brushed it off and found it was a baby gecko. The mother was giving birth on the ceiling. The baby was dazed for a little while, but soon recovered and ran up the wall. Another time, I put some eggs on to boil in the teakettle and out of the spout popped a gecko. It was quite a surprise for both of us. It was also the season of frogs. There were hundreds, and we reluctantly got used to squishing them underfoot when we went out at night. The roaches were two or three inches long, and were formidable-looking but shy.

Christmas came during our month in the school. We were taken back to the President Hotel to celebrate. On Christmas day, a friend came to my room and asked how I was doing. I said, "Just fine," and then started to sob. So I got a hug and a dinner invitation. Most of us were glad to be in Fiji, but sorry to be away from our families at Christmas.

We continued with our classes until it was time to go to our families. Two weeks living with a Fijian and an Indian family were a part of our training. The Indian towns are called settlements and the Fijian towns, villages. My first experience was with an Indian family. The father had a general store and some rice fields. The family was considered well-to-do. There were seven members in the family: the father, a married daughter, Mrs. Naidu, with her husband and two children, two older daughters and two grown sons. The boys helped with the farm and the store. Mrs. Naidu was there to take care of her father while the "Mum" of the family was in Canada helping a married daughter with a new baby. The children called me "Paati" which is grandmother. I liked that.

There were several rooms in their house, and I shared a bedroom with the two older daughters. One worked in Suva and spoke some English. The family was very religious, and one room was set aside as a shrine with pictures of Hindu saints. The altar was decorated with tinsel and bright colored paper. The father fasted all day and we had late afternoon prayers. It was all in Hindi and I didn't understand a word, but the loving spirit shown helped me to pray and meditate. Some food and milk was placed on the altar in the morning. After the prayers, the food was blessed and we each had some. The milk, which had been on the altar since morning, was poured into our palm and then drunk. As a nurse, I worried a little about that, but we all stayed healthy.

The kitchen was the most interesting room in the house and the center of social activity. It had a beaten earth floor. Chickens, ducks, and other animals walked in and out although this was technically not allowed. The cooking was done in a fireplace with a wood fire. Mrs. Naidu was the cook. She got up at about 5:00 AM to make the fire and do the day's cooking because it was too hot later in the day. There was always a curry made of some vegetables grown on the grounds such as bread fruit, squash, or pumpkin. *Dahl*, a split pea, lentil, and rice soup was made daily. This supplied the protein. *Roti*, a large, flat, unleavened bread, was baked on a grill over the fire. A piece of it was used to scoop up the food. I found it hard at first to eat without utensils, but got quite good at it. In the morning, before I walked along the river to school, a mile away, Mrs. Naidu prepared a parcel for my lunch. This was a roti filled with curry, folded over, and then wrapped in a newspaper. I put on my backpack, and my shoes which were outside the door, and started my walk along the river to class. Other Peace Corps volunteers joined me from their homes along the way. When we met Indian people along the way, we always did a "namaste." To do this, you put your palms together at your heart, bow your head, and say the word. It means in Hindi, "I greet the god within you from the god within me." I liked it.

All our teachers were Indian and were very good. We had a number of classes from eight until noon. We studied the culture, geography, agriculture and language of the area. At noon, we met to open our parcels for lunch. We also usually bought a lemon smash at my "father's" store. I got some fruit at the open-air market. The fruit grows all around and I couldn't understand why the local people so seldom ate it. After lunch, we had cultural activities and time to be with our families.

During the afternoon, we could do tasks with the people, such as to hold plough handles, and walk behind a team of oxen, which we called Fiji tractors. Since this meant wading through thick mud as they were ploughing a rice paddy. I said, "No, thank you." One teacher took us over to the seashore to see the shells. They were unusual and very beautiful. We were told that a lot of the tides in this part of the Pacific converge on Fiji and bring these shells from islands all around.

We were invited to a Hindu wedding which takes place over three days. Everyone in the community and relatives from all over came and brought food and gifts. The women of the family dressed me in a lovely *sari* which had been brought over from India. They giggled a lot about my white tummy as they wrapped me in the sari. It was quite an honor to be offered this sari by the father who liked me even though we communicated only by smiles and translations by family members. They also lent me a pair of long gold earrings and a number of gold bracelets. I felt beautiful. The family wanted to have the best-dressed Peace Corps volunteer there and I thought I was.

Mrs. Naidu took me to a prayer meeting at the temple. She gave me some marigolds and camphor. She told me that you kneel, gather the things reverently in your hands, and place them on the altar before the statues of the gods. Then you do a namaste. The service was full of love and reverence. She also told me that when she prays, she prays for her family first, and then for everyone. She doesn't feel that the gods would listen to her if she didn't consider everyone. If that isn't a religious attitude, I don't understand what religion is about. I thought that there was no way in the world that one could pay for the experience I'm having here.

The brothers in the family wanted to practice English, but they spoke little, so I got a lot of practice listening to and trying out the Hindi I was learning. One thing I did learn happened when someone told a joke. They said he was "bahut bad mas" which meant very naughty. We had to pass a language test at the end of school, so all my speaking with my family helped. I learned a number of Hindi songs and chants to the local gods and goddesses, and sang them to pass my language test.

The worst part of the experience was the toilet which was a pit behind the house. It takes a lot of practice and fortitude to use this. I was the designated nurse for our group in the settlement, and one of the most persistent problems was constipation.

They have some strange health practices. There was a woman they feared had yellow fever. They were trying to heal it by stirring burning mustard in a brass bowl. I believe this woman had other problems, as we were told that there was no yellow fever, so I tried to get her to the clinic. Also, one of the brothers cut his foot quite badly on a rusty nail. I cleaned it up and bandaged it, but knew he needed a tetanus shot as he had never had one. I asked the family to help me convince him it was necessary, and he did decide to have it. It may save his life.

Let me tell you about Dannyboy, the family's small dog, who thought he was a lion or tiger or bear. He was so funny. He guarded me all the time, especially when I went to the toilet. Every once in a while he disappeared. They followed him to see what he was up to. He went to visit people where he got food and went to sleep in the most comfortable place in the house. They decided he was a reincarnation of Uncle Sacha who did the same thing.

About half-way through our time, the Peace Corps leader came out and had what he called colleague groups. They were held to give one another feedback and express our feelings about things. I had been feeling really high, but expressed my frustration about learning Hindi. I also realized how much I was missing my family. Several of us cried together a bit.

Our family got up early and I rolled my mosquito netting so no unfriendly critters could take up residence. Then I folded my top sheet and straightened my bottom sheet as I had been shown. I put on my robe and went out to the toilet and wash house for my cold shower. However, the women said that "at my age," I needed a warm bath. So every afternoon, they got out a baby tub they found some place and filled it with warm water that had been heated in a pot in the fireplace. I sat, with my knees up to my chin, and enjoyed every moment of my sensual luxury. It was one of the nicest parts of my day.

There are several expressions here which are commonly used. One is "javujavu," which means hurry up, and the other is "diridiri," which means slow down and take it easy. I decided that it was the time in my life to diridiri. We went to bed early because there is no electricity, and kerosene is "dear" - expensive.

Older people are honored here, and the family was very kind to me. They seemed truly sorry to see me go, and I was sorry to leave them. We shed some tears and promised to spend more time together while I was in Fiji. We did.

A bus picked us and our luggage up to take us back to the President Hotel. I felt a sense of adventure, wondering what would come next. It is always fun riding on a bus because there is so much to see that is new and different.

We then had a weekend back at the President Hotel to talk about our experience and to prepare for our next family visit, which for me was in a Fijian village.

While we were in Suva, I wanted to see the School of Nursing, so my friend John and I took a bus to Tamavua, where it is located. It's an amazing place on a high ridge of cliff. The drive is up a precipitous mountain road for about five miles. There we saw the school with some unimpressive buildings, but in a breathtaking setting. Suva is built on a peninsula, so you could see the ocean on one side, and the city and harbor on the other. It seemed to be the end of the line since everyone got out, but we wanted to ride back so stayed on. When I looked, I saw that it really was the end of the line—no road ahead. I said, "Look John, no road," and he said, "I shall remain calm." We watched with bated breath as the driver backed off into the underbrush, and maneuvered along the edge of the precipice, until he was heading toward town. Then all the people who had gotten off the bus hopped back on and we went to Suva.

The month I spent in the Fijian village was a far different experience. I was lodged with one of the poorest families in the village, by the luck of the draw. The father did a few odd jobs around the village and the food they ate was grown by the mother and other children. We all lived in one room. There were eight members of the family who lived there permanently, and a number of "big brothers" who came to eat and sleep. The boys partied far into the night playing music, singing, and drinking yaqona. I was given a cot while most members of the family slept on rush mats on the floor. I felt quite sleep-deprived because it seemed that the big red rooster under my window began to crow right after the music stopped. I hated that bird. The wooden shutters were closed at night to keep out the evil spirits, but I pushed open one next to my bed to throw rocks I had gathered at that rooster. I thought longingly of wringing his neck. I finally found a pair of ear plugs, and with that and yaqona, got some sleep.

They had a big grog party one night and as their honored guest, I had to match them drink for drink or they couldn't drink. I did get them to give me a smaller portion each time. The singers included a big, tall guy who had a high falsetto voice, and a tiny little fellow with a big, booming bass voice. The music was good, and the drinking was very ceremonial. The coconut shell or *bilo-* is dipped into the *tanoa* and then presented. After you take the cup, everyone *combos* (claps) three times. You drink it down and they clap again. When I was totally exhausted, I asked if I could leave. They said it was all right, but couldn't drink until I had disappeared behind my cloth shelter to bed. Then the party went on. I thought that this part of my stay could be called, "my life as a goldfish."

There was a piece of cloth that hung from a rope beside my cot so I had a place to dress, but most of the time, there were several children peeping under or around it. The children were all malnourished and coughed a lot.

I told the mother about the clinic nearby, but she had given up, and the father was too out of it to care. I liked the children and wished I could take them with me to be cleaned up, given health checks, and dewormed. There was one little girl, Vasava, who was sort of the Cinderella of the family. I believe she had a hip malformation. One night, when the father was not quite out of it with yaqona, he became annoyed with the boys next door who were playing too loud, He wakened little Vasava to go out in the rain, and tell them to quit. She and another little girl, Ana, slept beside my bed. About halfway through my time there, I almost lost it. I went over to the school house to cry by myself. There was no place to be alone where I lived. Luckily, one of my Peace Corps friends was there, and she held me in her arms until I cried it out. Then she cried, and I held her.

During the stay, one of the leaders came to check on us. When he saw the shape I was in, he offered to put me with some other family. As bad as it was, I couldn't do that to the family I was with. Their status was low and they needed the money. He gave me a hug and several jars of peanut butter that I had requested. I realized that I do want to be here in Fiji. That dedication did not waver. I was glad that I could feel as bad as I did and still want to be there.

There was a small side building where all cooking and eating was done. The meals were always *tavioka* and *dalo*, root crops which looked a bit like large carrots. They tasted like cardboard. They also had rice and tea. These things were eaten three times a day. The family was given eighty Fiji dollars to feed us for the two weeks. I asked for fruit as it grew all around, but which the Fijians rarely ate. I tried to stay with things that had rinds or shells because their sanitation was non-existent. They had been told to give me protein food so they gave me a piece of fish or a boiled egg every day. I found it hard to eat it with so many eyes watching every bite. I tried to share with the children, but the father would take it away from them. I found that in this very macho society, there was a strict hierarchy. The father came first, then the boys by age, then the mother, and girls got anything left. I did get some peanut butter to the little girls in secret.

They wash clothes by putting them in a tub of river water with some blue stuff which I guess is like "grandma's lye soap, good for pots and kettles, fer dirty dishes, fer yer face and fer your hands." Then they beat the hell out of them with clubs. They put some of my clothes in one day which I never wore again.

The shower was out back, and they put up a couple of boards which reached to my waist. I had to crouch down to wash myself. They bathe with their sulus on. The outhouse is called the *valle lailai*. It's the sort where you get in, squat, and then pour the water which you have brought with you into the aperture. The only nice thing about it was a big gardenia bush in full bloom right next to it.

One day, they took us on a nightmare trip up the river to get prawns. They took us in a boat for a while, but then put us out on a mud bank to gather the prawns. I slipped once and had to swim, but thankfully didn't get any of the water in my mouth. When I thought that the clams and prawns they eat come out of that ooze, downriver from another village, I could see why hepatitis is endemic. Even though I was protein-deprived, it was easy to refuse to eat them.

I soon had my first experience with "Fiji time." We were told to meet at the church at 7:00 PM. As I dressed, I realized that most of the family was still in the fields or the garden. All the Peace Corps folk were at the church at seven, but no Fijians. They arrived over the next hour or so, and the meeting began at about eight- thirty. We found that it was better to wait for the drum to begin beating. They had a large hollow ceremonial log called a *lali* which was used to call us or anyone to events. This drum is used in all Fijian villages.

Our lessons in Fijian culture and language continued in the mornings. The teachers were Fijian and nice, but not very interested. I passed my language test by singing "Silent Night" and "O come, All ye faithful" in Fijian. It seems that all Fijians like to sing and the music in church is beautiful. They have no instruments, but they sing in four-part harmony and with enthusiasm. They have some ukuleles and guitars for fun music.

They call me "kalo kalo," close in sound to Carol. It means star, and I like it. As I walk about the village, I hear, "Bula vinaka, kalo kalo." This means "a wonderful day to you, Carol." They like to hear me talk and laugh at my accent. Europeans (anyone white) that they have heard before were British.

The fruit is wonderful - mangos, papayas, pineapples, and bananas of many kinds. They are all around, ready to be picked. I found out how to eat a mango Fiji style. You rub it between your palms until it is soft, then poke a hole in the skin and suck the juice.

When we left, they cried. I told a friend that I thought it might be ceremonial, or they were sorry to lose the US dollars. She said she thought they were sad because we had a way to escape and they were stuck there. We were very glad to leave this village.

Then came the time for our group to separate and go to the places where we were to be posted. It was a sad time because most of us had grown to like one another. They had a ceremony in which we received our full Peace Corps credentials and were sworn in as full-fledged Peace Corps volunteers instead of trainees. I went out and bought a Swiss army knife and a flashlight as my reward. I was ready.

I was to be sent to the nursing school in Lautoka, across the island of Viti Levu. So I packed my things and left Suva. I found a place to live with a pleasant Indian woman, Mrs. Singh, who was about my age, and also had children and grandchildren. I liked it in Lautoka because it was a smaller city, and was on the dry side of the island. The good beaches were there too. I found the library, and a good Chinese restaurant. All in all, I decided this would be a fine place to live my two years in Fiji.

I got to know and like a lot of the teaching sisters at the Lautoka branch of the nursing school. They were all welcoming and showed me around the town. I was taken to the hospital which was built in this century, unlike the one in Suva. They started me right in with teaching in the OB ward. The students here not only deliver the babies, they suture up the episiotomies. This is necessary because when they finish school, they might have a whole island for which they would be responsible. They got me my Fijian sister's uniform which had epaulets. I had three red stripes on mine and thought I looked quite grand. At dinner, a couple of days later, Sister Litia said that she had to go to Suva on the following day to meet the Peace Corps person who was qualified in public health. She and that person would be working together in Suva. I told her that I might be that person because my master's degree was in public health. Several calls later the Peace Corps office called. I had been sent to the wrong place and was to come back to Suva right away. I said my sad goodbyes, packed, and left Lautoka. The Peace Corps does help one adapt to constant change.

Leaving Fijian Village

Fijian Woman washing clothes

Hindu Wedding

My Hindu Family

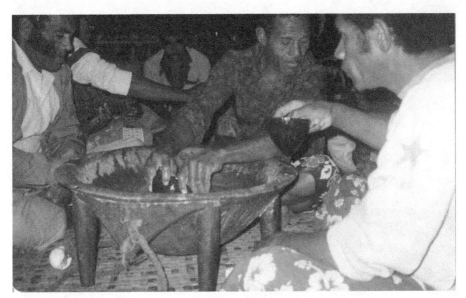

Yangona tanoa with Fijians

Fijian Drum "lali"

CAROL PHILLIPS

Fiji Tractors - Distributed by Caines Jannif Limited

CHAPTER 4

Places I Lived

AFTER TWO MONTHS of living out of a suitcase, I was ready to settle down and hang up my clothes. All the other Peace Corps had found living arrangements in Suva, so I moved to the nursing school sister's quarters. I felt sort of abused. When I moved in, I found it was quite posh. It had been an old army headquarters, and I was given the commanding officer's flat. It had a sitting room, bedroom, and bath which had a flush toilet, a huge tub, and a shower with a warm trickle of water. There was also a hot plate and small refrigerator accessible. They were rare here. In the other part of the building, there were four bedrooms. A very nice Fijian sister called Kiti Cocathanisigna lived in the one next to me. We had all the comforts left over from colonialism. I slept on linen sheets (patched neatly), ate on a linen table cloth, and had a napkin ring. We had a maid, Melenia, a 200-plus-pound Fijian. One day, she came in and found me singing and dancing to a tape. She came in right on the beat. She was my friend, and we communicated fine because we liked one another although she had no English, and my Fijian was sparse. If it rained she took my clothes off the line and folded them neatly. She put all our food, including the salads, in the warming oven three times a day. Some of the sandwiches we got are real surprises. Some of our meals included canned corn, canned spaghetti, and baked bean sandwiches. She worried that I didn't eat enough.

Kiti and I began to eat together, share the news of the day, and sit together to read in the evening. She liked to do crossword puzzles to improve her English, and we worked on them together. We settled down just like old friends. She had applied to a university in the U.S. and was accepted. Several months later when she left, I was sorry to lose such a good friend. I was glad that she got a chance to study abroad to further her career. We parted sadly. I began to look for other quarters.

Through a friend, I found a room in a house with a young British volunteer named Janet. She was from Liverpool. She worked as an occupational therapist in the mental hospital. The house was in a nice part of town called the Domain. The neighbors were mostly Brits and some people from other countries who were working in Fiji. Janet was the age of my youngest daughter, but we got along well. We respected one another's privacy, but enjoyed one another's company when we were together. We were both working hard, and had activities we were involved in. At one point, we kept hearing footfalls up in the attic. I told Janet that I thought we had rats or a mongoose in the attic. She thought it might be birds, but I said that I didn't know of any four footed birds. So we got the broom and took turns pounding on the ceiling. We also sang loudly. Whatever was in the attic eventually left. We both liked our geckos and our 12 by 24 inch refrigerator. Later another Brit named Helen moved in. There were only two bedrooms, so she made the living room her bedroom. Helen did not like Americans or older people, so we had little to do with one another. She had a very active social life and had parties which went on far into the night. Many of her male friends spent the night. This was not my business until a large Fijian man walked into the shower with me. It was clear that one of us was leaving, and I decided it would be me.

I met Allison who was a researcher at the University of the South Pacific on a shelling trip. She was working on a project about fresh water mollusks. She invited me on a trip up a river to collect them. I went and enjoyed the trip. We became friends and she told me that she would have to go to Hawaii for three months to do research there. She had bought a house in Suva and didn't like leaving it empty. When I told her about Helen, she asked me to move in. I did and we got along well until she left for Hawaii. I had not lived alone in Fiji and it felt a bit strange at first. The house was on the bus line, a great advantage. When she returned, I left because two women I liked wanted me to move in with them. It was for my good company, no doubt, but also to help pay the rent.

My Peace Corps librarian friend, Shirley, had moved into a three-bedroom apartment with an American woman we had met through the Rucksack Club. Her name was Jan. She had saved her money and had enough for a year in Fiji. They were an interesting pair because Shirley was quiet, careful, and methodical about everything she said and did. She was a fine lady who adapted herself to everyone else's needs, sometimes to her own detriment. She was trying to learn to be a little more outgoing and deal with life on a more spontaneous basis. Jan, on the other hand, was extraverted and a real talker. She announced when she was going to the bathroom. She was interesting and fun. I learned a lot living with them. We were supportive of one another when we had problems. It was also nice to have someone there who wanted to talk about what they had been doing, and hear about my adventures. This worked well until Jan ran out of money and had to go home. At the same time, Shirley's daughter came to spend a month, and they moved to a place together.

It was getting close to the end of my time in Fiji. My sister friends encouraged me to move to the sisters' quarters at the hospital. The building was like a beautiful old home and may have been the home of the colonial governors. My room was on the third floor. Just outside my room was a pair of enormous French doors leading onto a balcony with a lot of flowering plants. There were no screens, so the mynah and bulbul birds came in and out of my window. I had an incredibly bad bed. It had a wooden bar at the top and bottom. There were some strange metal pieces which ran horizontally and vertically. Even with a mattress, it went up at the head and foot, a lot like a hammock. Strangely, I slept better than I ever had in my life. Best of all was that I could lie in that bed, and look at the ocean. I enjoyed living with the sisters there until I left Fiji.

Me in Fijian uniform

CAROL PHILLIPS

CHAPTER 5

Varied Opportunities

THE PEACE CORPS had given me a job description when I was sworn in as a volunteer. A new curriculum had been written for the Fiji School of Nursing by the World Health Organization (WHO). My mandate was to help orient the Sister Tutors (British system) to the new curriculum and to teach classes while they went abroad for further schooling.

Early on, I was asked to give an orientation talk to the new nursing students. I was told to cover "Maslow's Hierarchy of Needs", Erickson's "Stages of Development" and "Man's Biological, Psychosocial, and Spiritual Needs". Then I was to help the students understand how nurses can use this information. I plunged in to prepare and suddenly realized the scope of what I had been asked to do. I told the person who asked me that this was at least three semesters' worth of material. She said she knew and that she was sure I'd be great. I poured facts and energy into it and I think it's the best lecture I've ever given. I asked her later if the students had gotten anything out of it. She said, "They liked it. I just wanted them to get used to your accent." At that point it was lucky I liked her

As time went by, I realized that the things in my job description were only part of what I was to do. Almost all health care in Fiji is done through the public health department as there were few doctors and none I knew in private practice. Most of the care including maternal and child health was done by nurses in clinics. Nurses also went into schools for health screening and preventive care. A student nurse had to be prepared to do all health care on an island after graduation. This would include maternal and child health and any 'stitching up' that needed to be done. Until the new curriculum, the students had worked only in the hospital and urban clinics. We were to augment a new project that took the students out into rural clinics to live with and learn from the nurses in residence. Since my master's degree was in public health I looked forward to working with this system.

I was also to do a number of classes with the sisters at the hospital. These were mainly in orientation to work in the School of Nursing, communication, interviewing skills, and motivating family planning. I was glad to meet the hospital staff. The nurses I worked with in Fiji were intelligent, caring and enthusiastic.

An early class I taught was on communication. In the class were some wonderful ladies. We enjoyed the talks we had about new ideas in communication. On the day of one class, I had received a number of letters from my children. I was reading them and feeling sad at how much I was missing my family. I forgot about the time. The phone rang. It was the matron at the hospital telling me my class was there. I told her I was very sorry, and asked if we could set up another time. It was set for two that afternoon. The first thing I said when I saw the class was, "When I didn't come this morning, I'm sure you thought 'I don't like this person. She doesn't care about me.' That is not true. I got some letters from my children and was thinking about them and my new grandchild coming. Do you think you can forgive me?" They all said with a smile, "Yes, kalo kalo." I went on to tell them that I was usually an optimistic person, but today I felt a bit sad. I told them that I didn't want them to think that my quietness was a lack of interest or concern for them. I used my behavior to start a conversation about nonverbal communication, which was our topic for the day. They participated enthusiastically. We had a good class with lots of hugs afterwards.

There were many more classes with this group and other hospital sisters. We all learned from one another. Some of them wrote a song for me which I treasured.

CHAPTER 6

Another Beginning

THE FIRST DAY at the nursing school was confusing and frustrating. I went to see the principal who was busy and couldn't see me. I decided to find some other Peace Corps people who could tell me what was going on. The people I found said they had never had an orientation, and didn't know what was wanted of them, so they were just sitting around. I got a copy of the new World Health Organization curriculum and read it all with the special emphasis on Public Health. The next morning, the principal was still busy, so I left a message that I was going to the school of Public Health. I really lucked out because I found a sister tutor there named Ilioi Rambuka, who took me under her wing. She had done a lot of work with the WHO people. She immediately sat down and worked out an orientation schedule for me. Since I was eager to get started, off we went.

She took me to several of the health centers. A model one was called *Lali Levu*. They had well equipped examining rooms and an up-to-date pharmacy. From there, we went to a more primitive one where I found out how much they are doing with what little they have. They have a system here from which health care everywhere could benefit. Each village has a volunteer health worker who is trained to go into the homes for health screening. They care for a number of what are called domiciliary patients with leprosy, tuberculosis, diabetes, and mental or rheumatic conditions. The volunteer worker goes into their home daily to check on how they are getting along. If there is a problem, she contacts the district nurse who visits once a week. For serious problems, a doctor is available for each group of villages. The doctor can admit the person to the hospital for a consultation. It's such a good system because everyone has direct access to health care. It costs fifty cents to go to the hospital. I checked the "family planning" supplies since I will be teaching that, and found that a month's supply of birth control pills costs ten cents as do a dozen condoms. The health care is subsidized by the government. The health care is good, if not by US standards.

One day, I went to the leprosy hospital. When I first went in, I kept my hands behind my back so I wouldn't touch anything. Dr.Dalako, a Fijian doctor, gave us a class in which we found that only 5% of people are susceptible to leprosy and then only on continued contact. I sat in on his clinic for a while and was impressed with the care he gives to each person. People can come in with any skin problem. He is so skilled that he can spot a person with leprosy on the street. He then tells them to come to the clinic. He said that when leprosy is found and immediately treated, the treatment time is only six weeks. The person can then go back to their home. They are checked daily at home and the nurse watches them take their medicine.

One of the things I found out is that our Dr. Dalako was a worldwide expert on leprosy. People come from all over the world to learn from him and he lectures in many places. The Center for Disease Control in Atlanta and the Leprosy Control Center in Louisiana maintain contact with him. There is leprosy at present in the United States because we have had so much immigration.

I went into the field as much as I could. I went to a number of health centers. It was exciting to go out with the mobile unit. It goes out every day to a different place. Several nurses go with it and they toot their horn as they go along, like the old time ice cream trucks. It goes to the poorer areas and the mothers bring their children out for worm medicine, check-ups, immunizations, and free milk. They get dried milk powder which the nurses tell them to mix into their tea. It is the only milk they get until they go to school where it is provided.

We also went over to a squatter village and looked around. The people who live in the squatter villages leave villages for the city and can't find work, so live a very primitive existence. The sanitary conditions are terrible. Almost all the toilets are pit toilets. The tide rises twice a day and spreads the effluvium. Garbage is thrown everywhere. They cook over fires and many have asthma from this. I met one woman who was coming home from the hospital after having a baby the day before. There was a straight-up path that she had to climb to get to her home. The husband took the baby and went up leaving her behind with a suitcase. I said, "Let me help you." I took her arm and the suitcase, and we went up. She just barely made it and had to stop to rest several times. When we got to the top of the hill, there was a woman who must have been her mother-in-law. It couldn't have been her mother. I asked her to get some water, and the new mother sat on a bench outside. The woman came with water, and I left, sadly.

I also went on a home visit with a zone nurse. I wanted to know exactly what they do well so I can teach about it wisely. The transport van took us, which was a luxury because the nurses usually have to travel on the bus. We walked through the village for about half a mile before we got to the patient's bure. We took our shoes off outside the door. There was a dirt floor with mats on it. We were visiting an elderly lady who had had a stroke. She had been home from the hospital for several days and we were checking on her progress. We sat on the floor and talked to the daughter-in-law. The patient was aphasic and the daughter-in-law was caring for her. Apparently, she was such a mean old woman that her own daughters had nothing to do with her. They nail the door shut at night so she won't go out, wander, and hurt herself. During the day, however, some member of the family stays with her. The kids sing "langasera" (hymns) to her and she seems to love that. One of the little three-year-olds was there and the grandmother petted him. We sat and talked for a long time. She had on a polyester dress to which I pointed and said, "kata, kata, muy kata kata" which means very hot. The daughter- in-law who spoke no English said that they had just bathed her and dressed her in that because we were coming and they wanted her to look good. The sister translated for me. I asked, "Sulu?" And she nodded yes. Sulus are what we all wear around the house because they are so comfortable. It's a length of cloth which is wrapped around the body. The caretaker said the patient did wear sulus when they weren't expecting important people like us.

I liked everyone I worked with. The public health nurses seemed dedicated, smart, and were doing a good job. The one I worked with most closely was named Eloi Rambuka. She was a wonderful lady, full of enthusiasm and first hand knowledge. She and I worked well together, and I learned a lot from her.

I finally got to see the principal. She was an Aussie lady who had been seconded to the school of nursing to help get things shaped up. We discussed the project which was to have been started last year, but had been put off. She asked me to write up a proposal with an outline of what needed to be done. The basic idea was to start beginning students with a multi-problem family, which they would follow for the three years they were in school. Few of the people in Fiji connected what they ate or hygiene with their health. I guessed I'd have to convince the students first because I'd already seen that they didn't believe in the germ theory. Since I'd been interested in preventive health care since graduate school, I knew I'd really enjoy working with this. There was a six-week urban attachment to the health centers which was already in operation. During this, we added scheduled visits to the school for the blind, orphanage, crippled children's hospital and old people's homes. I had to create worksheets so the students could report on what they found. Also, on what they thought could be done to help. The part that was most demanding was creating what is needed to begin the rural attachment for the students. We set up workshops for the nurses in the rural health centers so they could know what we expected in teaching and supervision. It helped them to accept students when they knew we valued their help. It is imperative for the students to have this experience because a number of them will be sent to an island where they will be in charge of all the health care including labor and delivery, school care, and stitching up. This will be our big project.

As time went by, I began to develop the other classes which were mandated by the WHO. These were research and epidemiology. I had some trouble teaching the students about research at first. I wanted them to understand that research can be used to help patients. As time went on, they got interested and developed some interesting projects. One was to find out the effect of the number of prenatal visits by the mother on the birth weight of the baby. Another, which the tutors in the hospital didn't like, was to record the amount of time it took the tutor to come when the student asked for help. They continued to use research methods in many ways. I was proud of them. I worked hard to make the class in epidemiology interesting and useful for the students. I had to relearn all the material for myself starting with standard deviations and square roots. I had my doubts about this class, but did my best to get an outline and some worksheets ready. It was to be taught after I left, and I hope that the sister tutor who did it had gotten informed about it overseas.

CHAPTER 7

Students

THE STUDENTS WERE a delight. I taught classes at all three levels, so got really attached to many of them. There were about an equal number of Fijian and Indian students. There were ten men. It was such fun to walk into the classroom, and have them all stand up, and say "Gud Morning, Seesta." They know how much I like them so there was usually a group hanging out in my office. It's such fun to see them as human beings, and not simply students. One day a male student said, "Oh, Seesta, we're always so glad when you are our teacher because we know we will have an interesting, exciting class. We talk a lot about the sister tutors and we like you best." I told him that I liked them all too, and was glad that my joy in teaching them and interest in the subject matter were coming across. They are interested in life in the United States, and we talk about that as well. The students loved to party, and included me in many of their activities. One party I remember well was an entertainment they put on for the sisters. It started with several of the Indian girls in beautiful saris doing some of their traditional dances. Then a group of Fijian girls did a *meke*, which was acting out a Bible story. It was a series of chants; some solo and some the whole group. One of the girls had written it. I found out it was about Moses. Then they began a *tarala*, a dance in which they begin the steps and then bring in everyone. I enjoyed dancing with them.

I rarely had to discipline them. I once gave them a real dressing down and apologized afterwards for losing my temper. They said, "Oh, Seesta, we know that it's because you are caring of us."

There is an interesting process here called "gating." I never did figure out the full meaning, but part of the discipline is that they can't go out during regular dating times. One of the girls who had just gotten off gating came in on Monday morning, and said to the principal, "Please put me back on gating because I've been naughty." I don't know how naughty she really was. I have been telling the girls personally and in the classes that they can choose not to have sex, but if they do, to use protection. If a student does get pregnant, she is dismissed from the school immediately and I don't want to lose any of them.

The tests they had to take were laid out on their desks before they came in. One day, when I went to put out the tests, I saw that the maid had put a little bouquet on each desk. I'm sure that can only happen in Fiji.

As I was grading the tests on medicine and surgery, I found a number of answers that I wanted to keep. The students did poorly on the psychological aspects of preparing people for surgery. Some of the answers were, "Almost everyone lives through this surgery," "Your surgeon is pretty good," "You won't have problems anymore," and "don't tell them any bad news like your wife just ran away with another man." Many of the answers were really creative. One person wrote, "To comfort the bereaved family of a person who has died, get the family in, and tell them to cheer the patient up." I made a note on the paper that since the patient was dead, this was not possible. Other comforting thoughts were, "It's a good thing he's gone because he isn't suffering anymore," and "the nurses and doctors did the best they could but they failed." I realized that I had to do a much better job helping them to understand this material.

Another test was on helping people accept the need for family planning. One answer was, "Make the age for marriage later, and sex after marriage should be made compulsory." The student who used that word didn't have a clue about its meaning, but I had used it and they liked it. To a question about what in the culture made people reject family planning, one answer was, "God gives children, so we take it." Another answer, "Fijians are great followers of Christianship"" I asked them to give an example of an open-ended question. The prize winning answer was "the digestive system." That certainly is open-ended I will have to work on that. Then I asked for a fact as different from an opinion. The answer, "God exists," had me stymied. When I asked them to define "thinking," one answer was, "it has something to do with the future." I loved them all.

Students

Students

Student party

Students in Class

CAROL PHILLIPS

Nursing School—all classes

CHAPTER 8

A Note on Graduation

WHEN THE STUDENTS come up to get their diplomas, their mothers wait at the foot of the steps, and put a lei or garland around their necks. The first year it put me in tears, but later I could just enjoy it. The students curtsey to the director of nursing, curtsey to the lady who pins on their nursing pins, and then turn and curtsey to the audience. It's touching. We had the usual crises. Two of the students couldn't find their epaulets. They get a blue stripe added when they are graduated. These two also couldn't find their caps, so there was much dashing about. We finally found the missing items so they were all properly dressed to enter. Many of the students make their own uniforms because although they are issued uniforms by the government, they are made for Fijians and largish Fijians. Size 3 is made to fit someone who weighs about 150 pounds. So the tiny little Indian girls all make their own. They were of all lengths and tightness. I was glad that no one's slip was showing, and said as much to my sister friend sitting next to me. She said, "Just wait," and sure enough, the next person had on a black slip showing. I said, "Oh no," and she said, "don't fuss, she usually doesn't wear one at all." One of the top students, who had won a prize, had on the government-issue shoes. They were 3 or 4 sizes too large. She said, "Oh sister, I hope I can get up the steps." So we stuffed the toes with cotton and the heels with toilet paper. She did fine going up and down the stairs, and I was really proud of her.

The minister of health was the speaker for the day. He had a crutch because he had just come back from Australia for what they call "getting spare parts" for knee trouble. It's not much of a vote of confidence for the Minister of Health of Fiji to go to Australia for health care, but was probably prudent. I was sitting behind him and noticed them changing the cushions on his chair before he sat down. When he got settled, I saw a drip coming from the ceiling. I didn't know, and didn't want to know, where it was coming from because it wasn't raining. It was dripping right on his bald head. It wasn't dripping fast, perhaps a drop every ten seconds. I was fascinated. Someone gave him a garland, and he moved his head, so it was dripping on the garland. When he got up to give his speech, they moved his chair, and he was finally drip free. He gave a nice talk to the students.

Students at Graduation

CAROL PHILLIPS

CHAPTER 9

Classroom Teaching

MY CLASSROOM TEACHING, which I really loved, was often team-teaching classes with the sisters who were going off to other countries until they left, and then taking over the class while they were gone. The sisters with whom I worked were dedicated and interesting. We learned from one another. The first class I taught was about family planning and family welfare from the public health point of view. An important part of it is the experience for the students out in the clinics. Sister Litia was the main public health sister involved in the project, and it was a real pleasure to work with her. We bounced ideas off of one another and would finally come up with a workable consensus from which we could plan. We worked together in the classroom and in the field.

A Sister tutor with whom I really enjoyed teaching was Mariani Takana. She was a wonderful lady and an experienced public health nurse, but had never taught student nurses before. She laughed at me because I ate pumpkin seeds and dried mango. One day, I had prunes and offered her one. She said, "Oh kalo, I'm going to miss you so when you go." After she taught her first class she asked, "How did I do?" I said, "You are a natural, you were great." She asked, "How could I be better?" I told her that she was used to dealing with experienced nurses so she thinks that the student nurses know more than they do. She also let the students run away with her, and here they think that if you don't discipline them, you don't really care about them. We talked about these things. We had a heavy schedule because the class we taught was from 11:30 AM until 3:00 PM. We were also teaching for four hours the next day. I don't really mind because we were teaching the second year students, and I was very attached to them after working with them from the beginning.

One day, I had the students for a class about occupational health and safety. A neighbor of mine was the head of the Ministry of Labor, and I asked him if I could bring my students to the ministry. He has written the legislation about labor and is very knowledgeable. We spent the whole morning with him. He had a lot of good videos, and was an interesting speaker. I hope the students learned as much as I did. In the afternoon, he had set up a field trip to the public works department. We got to see the heavy machinery and the safety measures they use for them. Then we went out to the docks and got to see the equipment they use for loading and unloading the boats, and how they are used safely. He asked if we would like to see the Fiji Bitter Brewery, and I said we would. It was an interesting process and the students really enjoyed it all. Knowing the head of the ministry gave us a great day. I'll try to set it up for the future classes.

Working with the other sister tutors was a joy. We had regular meetings to discuss the curriculum, class schedules, and the numerous things necessary to keep the school going. We had a good time since there was a friendly spirit in which ideas could be discussed. They included me as a member of the group. They were intelligent, enthusiastic, and caring people. Some invited me to their homes to meet their families. I was sort of an honorary Fijian and liked that.

Part of my job was going to all the urban health centers to see how the students were doing. It is good public relations for the school, as well as fun for me, to have a working relationship with the nurses in the field. They are much more cooperative with our goals for the students when we work with them. I could do a better job teaching when I had been with them in their work places.

I was happy with my work and stayed up beat most of the time. Occasionally I had to stop and keep remembering my role, which was to be a resource person and not "save the world." When I saw things undone it was hard for me to sit and let things be chaotic. I had to break the habits of a lifetime. It wasn't considered nice to be pushy and get things done. So I watched while appointments were not met and everything inched along on Fiji time. My evolution sent me to Fiji and this was one of the important things I had to learn. I don't have to be useful every minute to earn my daily breath. I know that in my mind. If Fiji can't put it into my body and spirit, nothing can.

After a lot of planning and hard work, the rural attachments were in place. Many of the health stations were in remote areas. We took the students out to each health station and stayed while they got to know the nurses who worked there. We had previously worked with the nurses to let them know what we expected. The students had work sheets to help focus their learning. The health center was always in a village. We were glad to see that the people in the villages came to meet the students and welcomed them. We found that the students became part of the community.

Hospital Class

CHAPTER 10

Rural Attachment Adventures

TAKING THE STUDENTS to the remote health stations was quite an adventure for me. My dear friend and fellow worker in the project, Sister Litia, knew the country and the people so doing it with her was a joy. We had a four-wheel-drive jeep; and when travel on the road was no longer possible, we rode horses, or walked. Once, we had to cross a river but didn't know how deep the water was, so Sister Litia walked ahead through the river to find the shallow places. I followed her in the jeep. We made it nicely. It was always necessary to look out for cows, chickens, or other animals that wandered on and off the road. There are no grange laws.

On one trip, we drove up the Sigatoka River valley. It was beautiful country. They call it the "salad bowl" of Fiji because crops grow so well there. The land is dark and rich. The locals told us that during hurricanes, it's the mud bowl of Fiji because everything gets wiped out. There is some way in which the winds roar through the other mountain valleys, and funnel wildly into the Sigatoka valley.

They put us up at the nursing stations, which were usually in a small valley at the top of a mountain. It was so pretty because in the morning, you could see the fog in the lower valleys, which I'm sure looked like clouds to the folk down there. The air was crisp and cool, a real treat after the heat, and humidity of Suva. It was nice to see dew on the grass in the morning.

One of the nursing stations we visited was in a village called Korolevu. It is in the very center of Viti Levu. There are myths saying that all Fijians come out of that center. It's a beautiful village that can only be reached by four-wheel-drive, horseback or on foot. All the children rode to school on horseback. The Doctor came to the clinic one day a month on horseback. The roads were bad with some straight up, or down places, and a lot of hairpin curves. We were glad to have our jeep.

Some of the nursing stations had a bed for us, but in one we bedded down on the floor on our woven mats. We had a small thatched- roofed bure of our own. It was cold that night and I wrapped up in everything I had with me. I lay down with my head in one corner. My friend, Litia, had her head in the center where the wind was blowing over it. I asked her why, and she didn't want to tell me, but finally did when I kept asking. She explained that if one's feet were exposed, the evil spirits could enter the body through the toes. She was one of the most intelligent and well-educated nurses in Fiji. So I told her that if any evil spirits entered, I hoped they would come and keep me warm. She didn't mind me saying that, but it didn't change her mind or her sleeping position.

At one station, on top of a mountain, in the deep interior, we spent the day working with the students and the resident nurses. After dinner, we sat on mats outside. My Fijian wasn't very fluent, so as it got dark, I lay back on my mat and watched the stars. Litia was talking to the staff nurse and telling her how to deal with some of the things she needed to know. She was also telling her how to clean up her act. Litia does this so kindly and with humor that the person feels good about it. While this was going on, the stars were putting on an incredible show. There was no electricity anywhere around to spoil things. Each star was bright and some were brighter. There were a number of meteors. Litia said she saw one I missed, which went across the whole sky with some little ones trailing along behind. I felt very close to heaven on earth.

Nursing Station

4 wheel Jeep Roads

CHAPTER 11

Personal Health in Fiji

OUR OWN HEALTH in Fiji was an issue we all had to deal with. Hepatitis is endemic, so we were all given immune globulin every four months. Germs, as well as everything else, grew profusely on our side of the island, which was hot and damp. I had one coral scrape on my ankle, which became badly infected and had to be treated with antibiotics. At the beginning, I had many bouts with guardia, which is an intestinal parasite. I was treated for it, but had lots of cramps and discomfort. I began to boil all my water, and took jugs of it with me on any trip I took. It was also necessary to wash all food carefully, and peel when it was possible.

The welcome yaqona ceremony, which is mandatory, gave me my first cleanliness concern. The root of the yaqona plant is dried and pounded into a powder. This is then mixed with water for the ceremony. The water and powder are mixed by hand. This is repeated until the desired taste happens. My concern was that I never saw a Fijian wash their hands in two years.

This was also a problem in my nursing instruction as I was not able to help them understand "sterile." If a thing had been boiled once, it was sterile, even though it had been dropped on the floor. When I had a blood test done as I was leaving, I saw the nurse put her finger on the needle just as she was inserting it. It was too late then for me, but I quietly told her to guide the needle in by just looking at it in the future.

I broke a bone in my hand while washing clothes. I didn't know it was broken, and thought the pain and swelling would go away. A couple of days later, one of my fellow teachers said "Kalo, you look like you have elephantiasis." That sent me to the clinic to see the doctor who said it couldn't be broken because I didn't jump enough when he touched it. The next day the Peace Corps nurse happened by and asked what happened. I told her that I had hurt it, and it didn't seem to be healing well. She told me to get in her car and took me down to the office to have an X-ray done.

It was a break, and I had to wear a splint for a while. Strange health care. We had all decided, early on, that if anything serious happened, we would take the first plane home. All in all, I was pretty healthy during my two years in Fiji.

CHAPTER 12

Travel in Fiji

TRAVEL IN FIJI was always an adventure. We walked to most places. There were few cars, probably less than fifty in the country. People depended on buses to take them any distance. Few roads were paved, and bridges were rickety. If the bridge looked too bad, we got off the bus which traversed the bridge. Then we walked over, and and reboarded . If an Indian was driving, there was a good chance of getting to a destination in a reasonable time. If the driver was a Fijian, he might want to take a nap, or wait for a friend, or relative to get to the bus. I always took a book. One day as I was waiting, the driver's rear view mirror slipped down. I looked at all those beautiful, strong, dark faces reflected there. Then I saw a pale, wan-looking person and thought, 'they may need a transfusion'. It was me. When we traveled to the other islands, we usually hired a boat of some kind. We rarely flew because that was an adventure of its own. One had to be weighed and leave behind any luggage that exceeded the weight allowed.

The Rucksack Club was made up of a number of people who had been *secunded* to Fiji. To be secunded meant that they were hired by their government with a part of their salary paid. The rest of their salary was paid by the Fijian government. The Fijians asked for independence from UK and were given independence in 1976. The Fijians had never learned how to do the things that make a country run, so asked for help. The people who came to work and teach the Fijians were mainly from UK, Australia, and New Zealand.

Holidays in Fiji were wonderful because they were all four-day weekends. Since we celebrated not only all the Christian holidays, but Diwali, Mohammad's birthday, Queen Elizabeth's birthday, and Prince Charles's birthday, we had a lot of long weekends to travel. They skipped the 4th of July and thanksgiving, of course. I did have one delightful thanksgiving dinner with a family from the American Embassy. They brought a turkey from Hawaii in dry ice and had all the trimmings.

I was welcomed as a member of the Rucksack club, and made lots of interesting friends as we traveled. A number of the resorts on Viti Levu enjoyed the business of the ex-pats and took pity on the Peace Corps, so we made good use of their facilities. To go to the other islands, we took a bus to the boat which we had engaged in advance. There had always been contact with the chief of the island, so we would be welcomed. There was a yaqona ceremony first, and then we were showed our place to sleep. We all brought sleeping bags since there were rarely beds.

On the trip to the island, Bega, there was a bure with bunks which felt very luxurious. This island was also one of the most interesting islands because it was where the Fijian firewalkers lived. Since we were there for the weekend, we got to see the whole procedure. They dug a pit about 10 feet wide and 30 feet long. It was filled with tinder and small sticks, which were lit and later the larger logs were added. When this was burning well, the pit was filled with rocks. This burned overnight. In the morning, the men who had prayed and fasted for some length of time came out and walked across the rocks. It was too hot for us to get close. No one who walked was burned. We were all awed. Then there was a feast of the food that had been cooking in another pit overnight. The fare was usually a pig and some fish which had been wrapped in banana leaves and covered with sand. The only green they ate was *bele*, a clover-like plant, which was cooked with coconut milk, and was tasty.

This was also the island at which we saw the giant clams. They were 4 or 5 feet across and we snorkelers were told to be very careful because if they closed on a person's foot, they did not let go, and when the tide came in, you just drowned.

A much less adventurous but interesting visit was to the US cable ship, which was often in Suva harbor. It traveled from Fiji to Hawaii laying and repairing cable for communication. The ship was one big computer with sensors which could find any breach in the cable, pull it aboard, and splice it. I asked the officer of the day what the crew does for entertainment as they are on the ship for long periods of time. He said they had video, and an open bar. My friend, Robert, whose father was the Queen's librarian asked, "Is there a book aboard?" The officer said, "Shall we resume the tour?"

The trip to Nananu-i Ra was fascinating. It is off the north coast of Viti Levu. We got on a bus at 6:30 on a Saturday morning. The trip took about four hours. It was 130 kilometers which is about 80 miles. This was on the King's Highway, which circles the east side of the island. It was a dirt road with deep ruts, so was a bumpy ride. It was quite exciting. We got on a ferry to the resort where we were staying which was delightful. There were eight of us, in the bure we were given. My bed was in a place where I could see the water which I love. The people were very interesting, and I met a few new members of the Rucksack group.

My friend Jan and I had an adventure on that island. I decided I'd like to walk around the island which I thought would take about three or four hours. Jan said she would go along. We started on a nice sandy beach but were soon having to walk around the mangrove tree roots, which grew down into the water, and around the rock formations, which were beautiful. I had on my sand shoes (sneakers), but Jan had on flip flops and was having a tough time. She finally said she had gone as far as she could go. I tried to support her but she said she couldn't move, and I had to get help. I left her sitting on some mangrove roots. I started walking through the water because there was a kind of bay. I held my camera over my head and wished I could just swim. It was about a half-mile across to a bure I had seen. A man came out, and with my halting Fijian, and gestures, I asked him if he had a boat because my friend, "that speck you see over there, hurt her foot and needs help." He showed me that he couldn't because his boat had too deep a draft. He had a friend in the next bure who he knew would like to help. We went to see the friend, and he and his two sons said they would like to do it much more than the tasks they were doing. We went back and picked up Jan. They took us back to our place. They said it was fun, and didn't want to take money, but we paid them. That island was a lot bigger around than I thought.

It was so nice because there was a mountain just behind the bures with a little valley at the top. It was very windy on the beach, but in that little hollow on top of the mountain, it was calm and serene. We went up there to read and laze, and look at the sky. The sunsets were spectacular. The moon was almost full and the beauty filled my heart.

Another interesting trip was to Naigani Island. It was about a two-hour-bus-ride to the Natovi landing, but as we went lurching along on the unpaved road, we heard a sound like a gunshot. It was a blown tire. The road was worse than most so we weren't surprised. We all got out into the mud while the driver fixed the tire. We were late but they had two boats waiting for us. There were thirty-four of us and one boat was for the gear.

It was dark when we got there and luckily, we had a good master to get us to the shore. On the last trip, the fellow we had, steered the boat with his big toe and took three passes to get through the reefs. This master let me sit in the fishing chair and enjoy the last red tinges of the sunset. They had dinghies to take us to shore from the bigger boat. The tide was out so they put us out into the water. I said to a new Peace Corps, "It's time to take off your shoes and roll up your pants." She said, "Surely not." So I got there with dry shoes and pants, and she didn't. It was interesting because coral is usually sharp but this was rounded and soft, and didn't cut our feet. It may have been old or dead coral. It was a nice resort and we all had a bed of our own. We had a wonderful weekend swimming, snorkeling and shelling. The rocks were especially interesting and beautiful on this island. The Fijians think some of the rock formations are holy places. I agree.

One of the best trips was to Kandavu Island. We flew from the Nausori airport through a rainbow. Only in Fiji. It was about a thirty-minute flight but ten hours by boat. We didn't want to waste a whole day on the island. Kandavu is a large mountainous island. There is only one flat place for the landing strip. It's less than a mile wide and not very long. You land and take off right over the ocean and trust Air New Zealand. I've gotten really good at packing; and can pack for a week in my straw Fijian bag. After we landed, we started walking along the edge of the airstrip, and then along the ocean to a mangrove swamp where we were to be picked up. There were punts-largish rowboats-out in the water to take us across. One of the Fijian men threw me over his shoulder, walked through the water, and put me gently into the punt. We crossed to the island, Maloa. It's a beautiful little island with a tiny village and the place we would be living. It is owned by a Fijian man and wife and their three sons. His not very Fijian name was Reese and the boys were William, Edward and Humphry. There must have been a European grandfather. They have a bure for themselves and a small wooden house where we stayed. Some of the Rucksack group brought tents. It was the Easter holiday so we had four days. They were full days because the generator went off at 8:30 PM, and we went to sleep. I grew to enjoy watching the dawn. There was an especially beautiful full moon, sunsets, looking at the ocean, swimming and snorkeling. I also found some beautiful rocks which they said were sacred. A wonderful place to meditate and pray. The snorkeling was special. I thought about the tropical fish I used to keep. This was like living in their world. There was one lovely yellow-green coral with little pink tips on each little branch. Among the corals were schools of angel fish. Above them was a cloud of tiny almost transparent fish which folded and flowed. The brilliant blue star fish were startling. I also saw sea slugs which look like short, fat snakes, but are not. If you pick them up, a stream of water comes out at one end. They are used for food, and at a Fijian dinner, where it was mandatory, I ate some. They taste like fishy jello.

On Easter Sunday, I thought I would go to church but found out it was a two-hour service in Fijian. William, friend John, and I took a boat around the corner of the island to a place that used to be one of the big stopping points for boats going from Australia and New Zealand to Hawaii. We went to an old village on a cliff which has gone back to nature. Will showed us some building blocks from the houses that were lived in in the early eighteen hundreds. He said, "You are walking on land right now on which no white man has walked for 100 years." I had a t-shirt that said, "The ultimate Fiji experience," for the cruise, but I felt that this was it. The ocean was rough on this side of the island because we were in a *winiwalu*, an eight-day wind, which happens now and then. I found some lovely shells in a little cave, and we climbed on the rocky outcrops.

When we got back to the village we sat outside the church and listened to the music. We heard the minister giving them hell. I heard 'yaqona' several times, so he might have been telling them to cut back on drinking so much.

There were so many things to do but we were so relaxed that we laughed about how much energy it took to get up, and saunter down to the beach to swim, or get up to find a book to read. The winiwalu kept it comfortably cool. The days flew by joyfully.

When we had to leave, the sea was so rough that they had to make three trips to get us back to the landing strip. The plane that came to get us wobbled from side to side, landed hard, and bounced a lot. I was a little scared because the wind was very strong and the landing strip was very short with the ocean right there. Once again, I decided not to worry about anything I couldn't change. William wanted to get to Suva so he sat in the copilot's seat because we had all the seats. Several Fijians sat on the floor. It took us longer to get back because we were flying against the wind and there was a lot of extra weight. I heard the pilot muttering about hoping there was enough fuel to get us home. There was.

The trip to the island Batiki was on a weekend during which we were celebrating the queen's birthday, so we got four wonderful days there. We left about ten o'clock on Friday night on a fifty-foot boat that some

Rucksack person had managed to get. It was very rough, and the boat pitched and tossed all night. We slept on the deck some of the time, and a number of people got seasick. Luckily, I don't. We got there at dawn and saw the sun come up on this beautiful island. There were about forty of us. We were welcomed on the nice sandy beach in front of the village. They showed us our sleeping bures. There were seven of us in mine. We walked across the island during the day and came back through some mountain passes. The views were magnificent.

I got to meet the chief's wife who told me that she had gone to Suva to visit her brother who was a policeman there, and met the chief. He was also a policeman at that time. Luckily, they both came from chiefly families because that is necessary for marriage. She is lovely and quite regal looking. She said that he had immediately fallen in love with her. He took a *taboa* (a whale's tooth), and traveled out to her family in the Lau group of Fiji to ask for permission to marry her. Permission was given. He came back to Suva and asked her and she said yes. They have been married for twenty years and have eight children. The young chief was very gracious to us. The old chief is bedridden, but still rules the roost. He doesn't allow any alcohol on the island, which helps because Fijian men can't handle alcohol. They get fighting and cane knives are sharp.

The first night, we were there, after the yaqona ceremony, they had a feast and a meke, the traditional dance which is done sitting down. Robert, who was our acting "chief" was supposed to give a speech. He said, "Thank you for having us and making us feel so welcome, vinaka vaka levu," and then sat down. They were very disappointed as they love long speeches. While we were there, we hiked over the lovely mountains and enjoyed the swimming and snorkeling. I hated to leave Batiki and they seemed sorry to see us go. On the way back, we ran into a storm and it was really rough. I took a *Dramamine*, found a hammock on deck, and slept in it most of the afternoon. I woke up only when it was so rough that I felt like I would fall out. We were rolling from side to side and front to back. Somehow, a Fijian man got up to the top deck and served us tea. We drank it and went back to sleep. We got to Suva harbor about 8:30 PM, tired from battling the storm but glad to be home.

There was only one source of electricity on Viti Levu. It was the Monosavu Dam hydroelectric plant, high in the mountains. The Rucksack Club couldn't miss that. We left on a Friday afternoon on a bus packed full of people and gear because we had to take food and bedding. I also had my 2 liters of boiled water because I had *guardia* so often when I drank the water. We took the King's highway which is two little unpaved ruts with lots of rocks for about 150 kilometers. Then we turned inland, and up the mountain. I do mean up. There were a lot of hairpin turns which the driver couldn't negotiate without backing up. At one point, we had a flat tire. We all got off and the men braced the bus so it wouldn't fall over the edge of the cliff. I was glad it was pitch dark. I had a bottle of wine and shared it. I thought, "Ho hum, I'm sure there is another spectacular view 2000 feet down." We got to the rest house about 1:00 AM. It had been built by the British and was nice. I was too tired the first night to unpack my foam rubber, and the floor felt like sleeping on bricks. The next day, a lot of the folk went to climb Mount Victoria, which is the largest mountain in Fiji. Several of us had the strength of character to stay behind and we had a lovely day hiking right there. We were on what is called the edge of the escarpment, a cliff from which the view was amazing. You could see about 100 kilometers. The villages looked tiny, and beyond them is the ocean and other islands. Driving down the mountain the next day was more of the same, but a little scarier during the day when you could see all the precipitous places. The driver drove all the way down the mountain in first gear. We got home.

I had been working hard, but when a new neighbor came over and asked me to spend the weekend in Ovalau, I said "Of course." The woman turned out to be a psychiatrist, and a very pleasant companion. It was an interesting trip starting with a ferry ride that took about four hours. Ovalau was the first capitol of Fiji and a large shipping center. We found a guesthouse owned by a Brit with a Fijian wife. They were very nice people. We got bed and breakfast for six dollars a night, right on the ocean, sort of unbelievable. We did a bit of mountain climbing and she shared my delight in the beauty of the island. We had to leave on Monday morning; the only ferry on that day. A good trip and a new friend.

A couple of friends and I had planned a trip to Vanua Levu on the new car ferry named the Princess Ashika. On the day we were to leave, there was a report that a hurricane, named Hina, might be coming our way, so the trip was postponed. Later we got word that the storm had veered off, so the trip was on and we went aboard. As soon as we got out of the harbor, the seas got very rough and the further we got, the more terrible the sea became. I've never traveled on water that tumultuous. Luckily, I don't get seasick. The ferry had flat ends, and with every wave that hit head on, the whole ship shuddered. Other waves were tipping us side to side. I sat out on a part of the deck which was covered so I was protected from the lashing of the rain. I just couldn't stay inside with my friends. The only problem was using the head because the pitching and tossing made it hard to walk, even holding on to whatever was available. The ship's engineer came up, and sat with me for a while, and said he had never seen such rough seas, which was not much comfort. What was supposed to be an eight-hour trip took twelve hours. When we landed at the village of Savusavu, I fell in love with it even in the rain. It's a tiny town right on the shore of a protected bay. The next morning, the storm had passed and we found out that we had indeed been in a part of Hurricane Hina. Exploring the town was fun because it took ten minutes to walk the whole main street. We left on the afternoon bus to go over to Lambasa, a larger town. We visited some friends there. A policeman told us the next day that Hina was coming back with winds of 100 mph and gusts of 160. We took the next bus back to Savusavu. It was raining but the real wind didn't start until evening. It blew hard all night, but by morning was just very windy and we went walking. It was wonderful. It seemed that at the last minute old Hina had turned away again, so the full force didn't hit Vanua Levu.

The seas were still too rough for Princess Ashika, and we were lucky enough to get seats on a plane back. We found that it had been much worse in Viti Levu as there was a lot of flooding and several lives lost. Never thought I'd ride out a hurricane on a ship.

The trip to Lautoka was not recreation, but part of my school duties. I went to chaperone a bus load of students who were going to their attachment at the Lautoka Hospital. I was told that we were leaving at 7 AM. I asked if that was Fiji time and they said no. I said, "really and truly" and the sister said she had heard that the latest we could leave would be 7:30 AM because they were expecting us for lunch. I went to where the bus was supposed to be and waited with my omnipresent book. At about eight o'clock, Mrs. Bakani, the principal, got there and told me we were leaving at about 9:30 AM. I told her we'd never make it for lunch and she said that they had prepared "cut lunches" for us to take along. They packed the bag lunches on the bus, full of roti, and curry parcels, and especially cream buns which the kids like. We finally got started a bit after 9:00 AM.

I noticed that the driver, Jak, who was an Indian had two gallon water jugs with him. I thought he must have diabetes and needed to drink a lot of water. Not so. When we had gotten about fifteen kilometers down the road, the steam started zooming out of the front of the bus. Jak pulled over and refilled the radiator from his jugs. Then he went to a well beside the road, refilled the jugs and off we chugged. One of the male Indian students, Taj had to stop now and then to get off and pee. Between Jak's radiator and Taj's bladder, we had to stop about ten times. We finally got to Sigatoka which is only 80 kilometers down the road about noon. The students there were on a rural attachment. My students wanted to stop and see their friends, so I said it was a good place to eat our lunches. They had all these big reunions. It had been two whole weeks since they had seen one another so there was lots of joyful hugging and exchanging news. It was lovely. After this and eating our lunches, we lurched on with the same crazy schedule as before. Luckily, I really enjoy the kids and they like me so we had fun. We finally got in about 4:00 PM and found that they had indeed expected us for lunch. They gave us what would have been our lunch for tea. It was a very nice tea.

A friend and I took a trip to Vanua Levu and Taveuni, which was called the "garden island" of Fiji. We were to go on the Princess Ashiki at 5:00 AM. We got to the pier at 4:30 AM, and there was no one in sight. When someone did come, they said she was to sail the next day. I went home and went to sleep, but my friend called and said she had booked us on a flight at 8:00 AM. We stayed at a place on Vanua Levu called the Kon-Tiki. It was on the ocean and quite beautiful. The man who ran it had a plantation and grew a lot of the food that was available to us. He went boar-hunting while we were there. A large boar had been eating the crops of a nearby village and had hurt several people. Our host killed the boar while we were there He showed us the jaw which had razor sharp tusks 4 or 5 inches long, The villagers came to thank him. He took us hiking in the forest and showed us many exotic and beautiful plants and birds. We saw one rare parrot whose picture was on the cover of the Fiji Bird Book.

We were to take the ferry over to Taveuni, and when we got to the dock, we were surprised to see that it was a tiny boat. I thought the ferry hadn't come in yet, but this was it. We got about half way across, with a heavy swell buffeting us about, when the engine quit. One of the crew, a real comedian, said, "Not to worry. We got a whole box of spare parts. When we get to shore we put one in. Last trip we ran out of petrol, but made it anyway." I didn't find that comforting because we were out on the open ocean between two islands. We couldn't stand up because the boat was rolling , but I got up on my knees to look over the side. I held on to the rail tightly. We were often almost horizontal. I was the only adult on deck with three Indian children. One of the kids kept moaning what sounded like "oy veh." The others were laughing. I said, "Anyone who understands the situation is scared right now. I'm scared, and he's scared, and you are weird." They laughed and said, "Whatever will be, will be." So I told them they were right and since my worry wouldn't change a thing, I'd laugh too. Eventually someone found a part that fit whatever was broken and the motor started. When we got to shore they went in stern first, so we had to leap into the water to get to shore. We were on Taveuni.

We found out why it was called the garden island. It rained for three days. We walked about looking at the town; what we could see between the raindrops. There were a number of beautiful birds which didn't mind the rain.

The most exciting part of our visit to Taveuni was going to the meridian. That is the 180-degree mark where you can stand with one foot in today and the other in tomorrow. I enjoyed that. After that we flew back to Viti Levu, glad to be home.

We had an interesting trip to an island called Vatulele. I had looked forward to it because we were to sail across on a ship called the Tui Tai. She was a beautiful white ship with eight bright orange sails. I had seen her but never been aboard. I'm not very good on measuring boats, but she was pretty big. We sailed and as soon as we got outside the reefs, the seas were pretty rough. It was a beautiful, sunny day. Luckily, I don't get seasick but a lot of people did. I was sorry to see all those Japanese honeymoon couples looking pale green and leaning over the rail. It was about a three-hour sail. We stopped on the beach, had a swim, and a picnic.

Then we went over to the village. When I saw the village, I was really discouraged. It's a community health nurses' nightmare. Everything that could be wrong was wrong. The water supply was polluted. If anything had fallen down it was just left there. They all walk about barefoot through animal feces and garbage, so surely have hookworm and every other sort of parasite. They probably don't have enough energy or feel well enough to do the things that are necessary. All the things that were bad in my village are worse here.

The single folk were assigned to what we called the "riffraff room." We had one big room with mats on the floor. I had a piece of foam rubber and

CAROL PHILLIPS

needed it. There were a lot of dogs scratching fleas all around. I was pretty miserable.

When we got to meet the people I got into a better spirit. We went to the school which was a broken down building with only a few seats. There were 173 children and four teachers. The books are old or totally inappropriate. I gave the school master ten dollars for a book which was about symphony orchestras and instruments. I thought he would use the money to buy some books the kids could use. After all these years, I wonder if I should have left it so they could see something beautiful of the outside world.

The Fijians have used only reed pipes and the human voice for music for many years. They have recently begun to play ukuleles and guitars. They do make very pleasant music with them. The drum is a hollow log, or *lali*. Some have improvised a sort of gut bucket, a string attached to a stick which is plucked. To them a symphony orchestra would be a mystery.

In this village they make *masi* or tapa cloth. They make it by peeling the bark of the mulberry tree. It is soaked and beaten thin before being spread out to dry. They then paint or stencil designs on it. It is very beautiful and I bought a lot to bring home to my family. We tried to spend as much money as we could because they need it so desperately.

We walked along a cliff to a jungle area. In the center of this, we found a number of caves with stalagmites and stalactites. In one of the caves, we saw the wonder of the island, the red prawns. They look like any other shrimp about four or five inches long. But they are bright red. The legend of them says that there was a Fijian princess who was being courted by a chief. He made these prawns different, gave them to her as a gift and won her hand. This is the only place in the world that they occur, so far as I have heard.

That night they had a *sevusevu* for us. To me, it seemed only a reason to start drinking yaqona. One of the Fijian women said that the men in the village don't do anything but sit and drink grog. It shows. The church was blown down during hurricane Oscar several years before. All the pieces are lying there as they fell. They meet for church in a corrugated tin shack.

The American Ambassador and his wife were on this trip. They had spent some time at the school so they could see how best to help. On Sunday afternoon, we got in a bit of bridge in their bure. It was the best one in the village. No dogs.

On the way back to the Tui Tai, I waded through some tidal pools. A lot of the kids came with me and we all played with the shells. They found me some lovely uninhabited ones. I paid them although they said it was just fun for them. They need the money and we tried to leave whatever we could.

We had a wonderful sail back on the Tui Tai even though the seas had gotten rougher. I was on the top deck and loved feeling the wind and the ocean spray. We sailed up the coast until sunset.

When we landed, the bus we had ordered wasn't there. In typical Fijian style, they had gone to the place where they had left us even though they had instructions and a map to the new place. It took them quite a while to find us. We waited and scratched our flea bites. Eventually, they picked us up and we got home tired and a bit grumpy. An interesting trip.

Chief of Batiki Island with wife, children and me

Pounding yangona on Kandavu Island

FIJI AND ME

Airport on Kandavu Island

Fijian Firewalkers on Bega Island

CAROL PHILLIPS

Fijian Firewalkers on Bega Island

King's highway bridge

CHAPTER 13

Recreation

THERE WERE SO many interesting things to do in addition to traveling. I often watched sunsets with friends, played bridge, and read books from the library of the old classics that the Brits had left behind. I tried to read one classic for every mystery story.

The people from the Rucksack Club invited me to a lot of their entertainments. The British had a drama group which I was asked to join. They put on a pantomime which was fun. At the first rehearsal, I found out that my partner for the dances was a pregnant female. She was the designated male, which I thought a little strange and offered to be the male. Anything goes in a pantomime, and she was happy with her part. Later, the dances got too strenuous for her so she quit; and I got a man for my dance partner. It was fun to sing and dance to corny old songs such as, "Oh, I love to sit beside the seaside." During one rehearsal, I told a friend from the British Embassy how wonderful and erudite the UK people sound when they read aloud. I felt I sounded a bit gauche. He said that since we had done all British plays for a long time, he thought we needed a change. He got a copy of "Guys and Dolls." We read it and laughed a lot. I tried out for the part of the "fairy of good intent" in a play. During tryouts, I gave a good reading, and then we had to sing. The Brits who sang, "Over the Rainbow" all seemed to have high, sort of squeaky voices. When it was my turn, I said I couldn't sing in a high key so I sang, "Send in the Clowns." I got the part and it was fun.

We got a new US Ambassador, and several of us were invited to a reception at his home. When I met him, I told him that it meant a lot to me to have someone who could really represent our country. I didn't tell him that I felt the last ambassador had been a turkey brain. He asked me if I'd like a tour of the place since he and his wife had just had a good-time redecorating. I said I'd love to. Queenie Nangasima, the new director of nursing, was there and asked if she could come too. He took us all around and showed us that a lot of the décor is built around some old quilts that have been in his wife's family. They were quite beautiful. He also had some nice American art. Queenie remarked that there was nothing from Fiji. He said that he liked Fijian things very much, but wanted to show the Fijian people some good American things. I thought this showed good sense and that the taxpayers' dollars were being wisely spent. He also showed us a pretty little pool house which he had made into a bridge room since there was a guest wing available. I told him that if he ever needed a fourth for bridge, I was available. He called his wife and said, "Get this lady's name, and address as a bridge player." I thought that I wouldn't hold my breath until I got that call. We did play bridge later on a Rucksack trip. This Ambassador and his wife joined in to the joys of Fiji. We did have one interesting interchange. He said that he had been in several places where there was unrest, and he was glad to be in Fiji which was so peaceful. I told him that there were a lot of problems in many areas between the Fijians and the Indians, and that I thought there would be open strife within five years. He said, "I'll bet there won't." I said, "How much?" He said, "Ten dollars." He still owes me ten.

Every Tuesday night the news was shown at the American Embassy. It was always two weeks old which was funny. A lot of us went to get together and compare notes. They served snacks, and we went out, and had a Fiji Bitter afterwards.

One day, when I was feeling a bit lonely, I went to see our volunteer director, Van. He was nice and funny, and always receptive to us. I told him that all my friends were away, and there was a good movie in town, and I didn't have anyone to go with. He said, "Have you considered that the new country director is your age, single, and probably lonely since he just got here?" I laughed and told him that I felt a schism between staff and volunteers. He said, "There isn't, he's in his office right now, but do as you please." Before I had a chance to think about it, I knocked on the director's door. We got through the hellos and how are yous, and I said, "There is a good movie in town. Would you like to go?" He said, "I don't think I am misinterpreting your invitation." I said that I thought it was pretty clear: would he like to see a movie. There was a long pause and he said, "Carol, I have not made a policy on this yet." I said, "OK, you will be missing a good movie." I went back to Van's office and told him what happened. He said, "I guess he is planning to run this country like an Army camp. That was bizarre." I agreed, but thought it was very funny. Interestingly enough, that man didn't last long in Fiji.

my non date

British Pantomime Bathing beauty

Fijians and me

CHAPTER 14

Friends

I'LL START WITH my friend, Mona, because we came to Fiji together; and were friends and coworkers in nursing through the two years we were there. She was about ten years older than I was, but full of energy and enthusiasm. She was right up front on every hike. She introduced me to a male friend when he came to Fiji on a visit. He was a doctor with whom she had worked for a long time in the states. His wife had died, and when he saw Mona again, he knew she was the woman for him. After his visit, he wrote, called, and begged her to marry him. She finally said, "Yes, if you will lose thirty pounds." She had been married three times before, and lost one husband to war, and two to heart attacks. She wanted to keep this one if they married. He did lose the weight, and they had a beautiful wedding. A Fijian friend sent a beautiful piece of tapa cloth for them to kneel on. I got to spread this on the altar and read the 100th Psalm. This was what the mother did, and I was proud to have that role. They were still happily married five years later when I visited them in California.

A person who felt like a friend, although I never knew his name was the preacher at the church I often attended. He was from Kiribas, a small island near Fiji. He conducted the services with such loving kindness that goodness radiated from him. He told a story one Sunday which sounded exactly like Plato's "Shadows of the Images." I was fascinated and wondered if these myths are so universal and true that they occur in all cultures.

Robert Austin was from UK but had lived in Fiji for some time. He was a writer. His Father had been a librarian for the Queen, so he was very, very British. He helped direct the Rucksack Club, and knew how to make arrangements for travel. He was often our designated "Head man" when we went to villages. He knew just how to talk to the chief. We had many good conversations about books and ideas. We often sat quietly and watched the sunset. He also had a fine collection of classical music to which we listened.

When I felt troubled or sad, I knew that Robert was there to understand and comfort me. A good friend.

Ted was from UK, but loved living in Fiji, and rarely went home. He was head of the Math department at the University of the South Pacific (USP). He was an avid and excellent bridge player. We had played some bridge on a Rucksack trip. One day, he called, and asked me to dinner, and bridge. The house in which he lived had a cat, which he had befriended and called Max. It came over to me, rubbed against me and got on my lap. It was clear to me that the cat was about ready to have kittens. I told Ted but he didn't believe it. As we were sipping our sherry, the cat began to make strange sounds. I said, "You better find a box and some newspaper." He did and the cat had four kittens. The dummy got to watch.

Ted never missed a Rucksack trip so we shared many adventures. We both enjoyed snorkeling and hiking. He took me to a number of events at USP. One of the new Peace Corps women said, "Ted asked me over for a cup of tea. Does that mean he is going to put a move on me?" I said, "If you go, you will get a good cup of tea, and interesting conversation." When his wife came, we played bridge and shared other activities. I visited UK later, and was invited to stay at their home which was a sheep farm near Exeter. It was quite beautiful and his wife loved it. He didn't really seem to feel at home there. He loved Fiji.

Tony was with the World Health Organization, and was a specialist in ports and shipping. He was in Fiji often, and came with the Rucksack group on many of our island visits. His home was in Australia, but he spent most of his time in the Pacific islands. I met him on Bega Island on a Rucksack visit. We had all been assigned bunks, but he was late. I told him that if he had the gear for it, he could sleep under my bunk. He did, and we talked until the other folk shut us up. Our conversations and friendship continued on Rucksack trips and over dinner when he was in town. He was a fellow Gemini, and we never ran out of things to talk about. He told me a story about his visit to Tonga. He went there to check out the Tonga Navy, but found that both boats had been taken around the island by the crown prince. They were having an extended picnic on the Tongan Navy boats. When Tony's wife came to visit, we did things together. Good friends.

You have heard about Kitti, my first roommate. I want to tell you something which shows how special a friend she was. One day, I was reading letters from my kids, and feeling really sad. Kitti came in and said, "What's the matter?" I boohooed and said how much I miss my kids and would like to be with them. She came over and hugged me; and put my head on her shoulder and let me cry as long as she thought I needed to. Then she said, "Now go wash your face."

Meeting Kim was wonderful. She came with a Peace Corps group just before I left. We spent many interesting hours together in the time we had. Her Peace Corps job description was to help the local women set up home industries. She was just out of college, but we spoke the same language, and had many ideas and ideals in common. We talked for hours about everything. We were sorry to part and she gave me my last hug before I got on the plane to come home.

Carolyn was a librarian in our group. We had meals and good talks. Carolyn found her job in Suva dull, and so had herself posted out to one of the outer islands to start a new library. We have corresponded through the years, and her son may come to Duke University.

John Young was from New Zealand. He was a law professor, but had been seconded to Fiji to help sort out the legal mess in the courts. His rather grand title was the "chief arbitrator." He dealt with the parliament and all of the courts. He was one of my neighbors. As we were talking one day, I told him that one of my frustrations in teaching in Fiji was that I couldn't make anyone believe in "cause-and-effect"-- that when one thing happens, another thing is put in motion. My examples were: "if you prepare food and wash dirty clothes in the same bowl, you will probably get sick." Another was, "if you drink water from the stream in which people upstream are bathing, and cows are wading, you may get hepatitis or typhoid which are endemic here." Later, John said that our talk had been a real help to him. He had not considered the cause-and-effect concept, and it had been a real help to him. He said it had changed his way of dealing with the people and issues. He now looked at Fiji as a culture that does not understand cause-and-effect, and was being much more successful. At the times I wonder if I'm doing any good here. I'll try to remember that I have changed the way the chief arbitrator deals with the legal life of Fiji.

Matron Tusiwanga was an interesting lady who dealt with many of the problems of the hospital. One day, she walked into my office which was a surprise because I'm up on the third floor, and don't get many visitors. I brought up the fact that there was a new post being created for the director of nursing. I know this matron to be well informed, fair, and intelligent. I told her that the one person who came into mind when I heard about this post was herself. She said that she had thought about it but that a woman seemed to want the job. In my opinion, this lady looked like a toad, and has about the same amount of brains as one, but I didn't say so. However she does have connections in the ministry so might have a chance. I told Matron Tusiwanga that it was very Fijian of her not to want to make waves or make anyone uncomfortable. I said, "It is very kind and thoughtful of you, but this position requires special skills which you have, and she doesn't." She said, "It will be as God wants it to be," and I replied, "God can't do a thing if you don't even apply for the post." She said that she hadn't thought of it that way. I asked if she might apply, and she said "I will." So I felt as if I had done something useful and good for the future of Fiji.

One of my friends was Sister Umbale Mabola. She came and talked to me about her husband's death. It had been 100 nights or about five months since he died. She was having a lot of pressure put on her to marry the governor general, whose wife had died, because she is of a chiefly family on a level with his. She is one of a very few people who could marry him. She was undecided because her husband had been a drinker and a carouser. He had been the minister of the Interior. She took good care of him, and the responsibilities which went with being his wife, but hadn't had a good experience with marriage. The man they want her to marry is completely different. We heard that his wife died of cancer. Her nurse said that he slept in a room near hers and whenever she would cry out in the night, he would come and hold her hand. He is a kind and loving man. Umbale kept asking me what I would do and would I marry him. I said "In a heartbeat. He sounds wonderful." But he wanted to marry her, not me. She then brought up his children who might not like her. I told her to give it time; spend time with him, and his children, and see if her feelings changed. We talked from time to time, and about six months later, she married him happily.

Ted with kids on Batiki

Mona and Jenner Wedding

People I lived with Kitti Me Matron Whippy

CAROL PHILLIPS

CHAPTER 15

Joan's Visit

ONE OF THE nicest things that happened to me in Fiji was my daughter Joan's visit. I met her at the airport in Nadi which is the only place where transpacific planes can land in the Fijis. It was early morning; and she had flown all night, so I took her to Lautoka to rest up a bit and meet my friends there. She bounced back in a hurry. She was twenty-five. The next day, we took the bus back to Nadi and looked around the town. She was as fascinated by all the different things to see and do as I had been. The following day, we boarded the ship for what was one of the most beautiful and exciting trips I've ever taken. It was a nice ship with about fifty people, from several countries, aboard. The crew did everything they could to make us comfortable.

Our first stop was the island where they filmed Blue Lagoon. There was a cave at the base of the cliff for swimming. I was too "chicken" to go into the second cave because one had to swim under water through a passageway to get to it. Joan went and loved it.

On Christmas Eve, we went ashore and had a picnic. It was lovely. There was a campfire, and we sat around it, and sang Christmas carols in our several languages. On the way back, the crew stopped the dinghies so we could look at the stars. I've never seen so many stars or seen them look so bright. We gazed in awe for a long time. At one point, as we drifted, I saw one especially bright star low on the horizon and said, "Wouldn't it be nice to go on to Bethlehem instead of back to the ship?" We all agreed that we would like that.

It couldn't have been a better trip. We sat up on the front of the deck and watched the ocean, the sky, and the islands we passed. We went ashore from time to time so Joan got to see a village with the *bures*, where people lived. They gave us a *meke* which is the singing, dancing, and *yaqona* ceremony which welcomes new people. She got a real feeling for the culture of Fiji through this Yasawa Island trip.

We got back on Christmas day and found we could get a ride back to Suva with some friends. On the way, they stopped at one of the big resorts which was owned by a friend of theirs, and had some lunch, and a swim. Father Christmas was coming in an outrigger canoe crewed by a group of warriors in the afternoon, but our friends had to go on, so we missed that pageant.

When we got back, I showed Joan my newest home and we settled in. Then we walked around Suva so I could show her the sights. We spent some time at the excellent museum with Fijian artifacts. We stopped at the Grand Hotel which has been the setting for a number of movies. That was the place for us to stop and have a *Fiji Bitter*, the local brew.

During the time she was there, we were invited to a number of parties where I was happy to show her off to my friends. I also took her to a jungle park that had been laid out by a Peace Corp person. You walk through the jungle beside a shallow river for three or four miles and come to a series of little pools. There's a rope over the last pool so you can swing out over the edge of the cliff and land in the water below. Joan did it. She didn't miss much.

We took long walks along the ocean and went to Pacific Harbour where she saw the Fijian fire walking. We swam in the resort pools which welcomed Peace Corps people.

On New Year's Eve, we went to a party for a while but weren't in a party mood, so we came home, talked awhile, and went to bed. At midnight, the fireworks started and there was no sleeping, so we got up, ate a banana, gave one another a hug and a kiss, and went back to bed, happy to be together to start the New Year.

On January first, we decided to go to the Coral Coast where you can walk on the reefs and snorkel. Before I went to Fiji, I thought that snorkeling was only for the " beautiful people". I found out that it's for anyone who enjoys water, and seeing all the wonderful things that live in the ocean. The water around the reefs at the Coral Coast is especially clear for snorkeling. The corals are all little live-beings that have mouths that open and close. When your face is in the water you can see the fish swimming all around you. If you are quiet, they come up and look you right in the eye. They seem to feel you are one of them. We were lucky enough to see a number of the brilliant blue starfish. I showed her some of the beautiful shells, but most were inhabited so we didn't take any.

I told Joan that one of the first things we are taught to avoid is the lion fish because if you step on one of their spines, they inject nasty venom. The black-and-white sea snakes are all around, but we were told that the fangs are in their throats, and who would put a finger in their mouth? The Fijian children play with them and don't ever seem to get hurt. We spent several delightful days there. We slept in a dorm and had a nice girl from Canada for a roommate.

The time went too fast and finally the day came when I had to take her to the airport. I hated to see her go, but the visit had been so good that my sadness was lessened by all the happy memories.

CHAPTER 16

Random Thoughts–some funny, unusual, wonderful things about Fiji.

THE PRESENTATION OF a whale's tooth—*Tabua* is a high honor given to visitors. A man is given the whole tooth on a woven chain. My students gave me a pendant with two pieces of carved whale tooth. I was honored and enjoy wearing it often.

The mail came in on a plane twice a week. We looked forward to it eagerly. While we usually got mail in a couple of weeks, anything could happen. I got a letter from my Mother sent on April 2 on July 23. One Christmas card sent on December 16 arrived in the middle of March.

All around the hospital in Suva are many shops for funeral directors and coffin makers. I saw one sign that said, "Funerals-Hearse Service-Furniture Makers-Joiners-Long Distance Movers." No matter where you want to go, that group will take care of you.

There was an Indian man named Vijay at the school of nursing who was a gardener and handyman. I always said, "Ce say, Vijay" or how's tricks and he replied, "Tik, tik, , acha" which means couldn't be better. I knew he didn't earn much and had a wife and three children. I asked him if his wife was more or less my size, and if she might like some dresses. He said she would and I gave him a box full. A week or so later he said, "My wife said thanks for the dresses and she would like a watch."

The Fijian idea of *kerikeri* is interesting. You have to be careful not to admire anything in a Fijian home because they will insist on giving it to you. However, that means that you must give them something of equal or greater value in return. It can get very complicated.

In the STD (Sexually Transmitted Disease) clinic lobby, they have a big welcome sign, "THERE IS PUNISHMENT FOR SIN, BUT GOD

FORGIVES THOSE WHO REPENT. SO GO FORTH AND SIN NO MORE." I always wondered if it did any good.

As I was walking by the hospital, a little Indian man came by in a pair of boxer shorts and a hospital gown. I asked him if he was from the medical ward as that was nearby. He said, "Yas, Seesta" So I said, "Why don't we go back, I'll walk with you. They might have missed you." When we got there, I found the nurse in charge and asked if this was one of her patients. She said he was, and they had looked all over for him because he had just gotten out of the coronary critical care unit. I told her I found him down the street and was glad I'd been there.

The windows and doors of the hospital are all open and there are no screens. On visiting days people come and lean in on the window sills.

Across the alley from the hospital pharmacy the "bottle man" had his display set up every day. He went all over town collecting bottles he found discarded on the street. He then rinsed them and sold them to patients who were getting liquid medicine at the pharmacy. They often didn't look very clean to me.

One day, one of my Fijian friends said, "*Kalo kalo*, a naughty bird has done something bad on the back of your uniform." When I went into the classroom, I told the sisters what had been said. They looked and said, "That's very good luck."

After I had been in Fiji for some time, one of my Fijian friends said approvingly, "You must have some Fijian blood. Look at how nice and brown your skin is; and the mosquitos won't bother you anymore." They were right about my good tan because I walked outside for miles almost every day. They were wrong about the mosquitos though, because I was often bitten.

Washing clothes in Fiji should be an Olympic sport. Sheets, towels, and everything was washed by hand, in wash tubs, using a scrub brush on a wash board. We used a blue soap which more or less dissolved in the cold water. You would wring the big pieces by winding them around a tree or fence post, then rinse them, wring again, and hang them out with pegs, which are what they call clothes pins. They were hung out in the morning and usually get an extra rinse from the rain. The nice ocean breeze dried them. I didn't feel they were very clean at first, but they smell fine from the rain and the sun.

The Indian shopkeepers pull you into their shops. I had to learn how to talk the talk. First you ask the price. When they tell you, you say, "Too dear"; and act as if you are going to walk out. After you are urged back into the shop, you offer about half of what they first asked. Eventually, if you really want whatever it is, you meet with a price some place in the middle. It got to be fun.

Viti Levu has a wet east-side where I live, and a dry west-side. The average rainfall where I live is 127 inches a year. The record for one day was twenty-two inches. We always had a light in the closet to help keep clothes dry.

Because of the International Date Line, Fiji always celebrated being first to bring in the New Year. We ignored Tonga even though it had a slight edge on us geographically.

The Fijian prime minister (PM) was quoted as saying "A lot of Fijians say, 'Get rid of the Indians, Fiji is for the Fijians,' but we cannot do that because if we did, we would sit down and not move. We need the Indians to spur us on to activity." That showed insight on the part of the PM.

In mango season, the fruit-bats come soaring in at sundown. They have a three-foot wingspan, and except for eating too many mangos that we want, they are peaceful, friendly creatures and quite beautiful to watch.

Raymond Burr, who played Perry Mason on TV, owned an island just off the coast. He grew orchids which were sent all over the world. I became friends with the people who managed the business. They had a greenhouse in Suva. They let us tour the greenhouse and gardens. Rare and beautiful orchids abound.

An Indian friend said that Fijian people don't understand mechanical things. The few who have a car don't think to oil or grease it. They drive the car until it quits and then take it to the garage and say, "Make it work," which is usually not possible. If a Fijian woman gets a car, she drives in the middle of the street and if anything gets in the way, she speeds up and toots her horn. They don't shift gears and you often hear a poor car grinding its way up or down a hill.

An interesting myth they have is that the first-born child can point the clouds away so it won't rain on them I tried it eight times and it worked every time. A friend asked if people look at me strangely while I'm doing my magic. Not in Fiji.

A little Indian girl, Shaleen Kumar, who lived next door, always walked to the bus with me. One day she said, "I come over to your house all the time but you never come to see me. My folks have gotten a special movie for you tonight. Please come." She looked so stricken when I made excuses that

I said I'd come. It was a very long movie and I understood about ten words. They watched me to be sure I was laughing at the right time. However, I was watching them even more closely to see when they laughed. It was quite grueling. The next day, I asked her to tell me what had been going on because I didn't fully understand. It took quite some time for her to explain. Believe me, a Hindi movie is quite an experience.

A very nice couple, the Collins, from my church in Durham came to visit. They had written that they would be staying across the island, but because of the last hurricane which had damaged a lot of the resorts, they were at a resort nearby. They called and asked if I'd come for dinner. Since it was only a short bus ride away, I said I'd love to. I met an interesting Fijian man on the bus. He was the police chief of Lautoka and had been educated in New Zealand. He was unhappy about the way he felt that Fiji had become dependent. He said that in the old days when a hurricane came, everyone got food and supplies and found a cave to shelter in. Now, when the hurricanes come, the Fijians start begging everyone for help. An unusual man.

When I got to the Pacific Harbour Resort, it was good to see my old friends. They were with a tour and I found myself a sort of celebrity. Everyone asked me questions and since I think Fiji is great, it was easy to talk about all the things I find so interesting. They seemed to think I was rather noble, but I told them that the only time I feel even a little bit noble is when I'm sloshing through the mud to get to the bus, or washing my sheets and towels in cold water on a washboard. It was a good visit. When it came time to leave, I went out to the road and luckily, a bus came by. I met another interesting man on this bus ride. He was a well-educated man who was a farmer because he liked farming. We had an interesting talk about crops. He gave me a ride home in a taxi because he was going to see his sister who lived in that direction.

My passport expired while I was in Fiji, and I went to the Embassy to get a new one. There were a lot of Indian people trying to get visas. This reminded me of something that happened to me awhile before. I was walking down the street and a young Indian man came up, and asked if he could walk with me. I said he could on this busy street. With the first step, he said, "I would like to marry you. I would take good care of you and never touch you. You could drink if you wanted to. I want to go the United States." I said, "That's interesting, but please let me tell you where you can apply for a visa at the American Embassy." I explained where to go, and we parted.

One day, when I was really wanting to be at home in the US with my family, I sat watching the sunset and thought it through. I decided that I had come to Fiji for adventure and spiritual growth. All the things I do at work and play are adventure. Being the only white person, and from a very different culture, helps my mind and spirit learn about other people and cultures—and about myself. I knew then that there is so much to learn and I was right where I wanted to be. Fiji.

One night when I was out walking, I heard a choir practicing in a church. I sat outside and listened. It was lovely. They were practicing the Messiah. It brought back happy memories of singing in many choirs. I went inside and found that there were twenty-seven big husky Fijian men and about fifty women. A wonderful choir singing beautiful music.

Most of the food I ate was purchased at the open-air market. All the folk with food to sell, sat on the ground with their food spread out in front of them. The Fijian food was mostly root crops. The Indians had more variety with pumpkins, squash, jackfruit, and all sorts of curries. The Chinese had the best things, oranges, tea, and local fruits we couldn't pick for ourselves. There was a small British shop which had canned goods, dry foods and other vegetables. Most of what they sold was too expensive for Peace Corps with our $240 a month income. A small head of lettuce cost $4, a stalk-not a bunch-of celery, 50 cents, and a box of cereal, $5. I asked about a small piece of broccoli which was $2 and thanked the clerk for letting me hold it. All the food I bought was packed into my rucksack to be carried home on my back. One day I thought, "Carol, you are a pack animal." Second thought, "What a healthy pack animal." Fish was selected from the boats down at the dock, but you only bought with a Fijian friend along because some of the fish were poisonous if not cooked in a very special way.

One day, we were sitting in the classroom and someone said, "Oh look, the minute-hand of the clock is going backwards." It was, and so was the second-hand on the big classroom clock. It was so satisfying because that's just what Fiji time is like.

My sister friends always want to hear about my trips. They tell me that I have been to more places in the islands than they have. I tell them that I have only two years and they have a lifetime.

You often see a woman sitting on a stool with a stack of coconuts around her. She cracks the coconut, saves the water, and puts the grated coconut into the container of water. Then, she mixes it, wrings out a handful of coconut, and puts it aside. This is used to feed animals. What's left is called coconut milk and is used to cook. I liked to drink the coconut water right out of the shell. There was always someone who would enjoy walking up a palm tree to toss down some coconuts. The cane knife sliced off just enough to make it a good drinking cup. During the ripening season when they were falling, you didn't sit under the trees and walked carefully beneath them.

The sisters had a nice birthday party with a cake and candles for my sixtieth birthday. I enjoyed it very much. My daughter, Janet, called to wish me a happy birthday and I told her that sixty sounded so old to me. She said that I should be like her Chinese friends who consider being older; a time to rejoice at the wisdom already gained and look forward at that which will come. A good way to think. I'm really too busy and interested in what I'm doing here to worry about it.

Most Fijians are large people. Many of the women are six feet tall and the men are even taller. A number of the men walk bent over in buses because they can't stand up straight. They are also heavy, but even the fat ones don't look fat. Their ancestors migrated from Melanesia and Polynesia. All of the Fijian men wear *sulus*. The dress ones wrap around and button. I think they are better looking and more practical than trousers. The women, since the missionaries, are covered from neck to toe. In public, they wear something called a *chumba,* which is a loose dress worn over a petticoat. At home, everyone wears a sulu as I do.

The Indian people come in all sizes but most are slightly built. All the Indian men wear trousers and the women wear *saris*. The Gujarati women wear a chemise *sawaal*. This is a loose, long-sleeved dress over trousers tied at the waist. There is also a shawl to cover one's head.

The clothes I got in Fiji came from one of two sources. First was Paddy's Market. I'm not sure where their nearly- new clothes came from, but they supplied my wardrobe nicely. For my uniforms or dress-up, there were Indian tailors. The one I chose had fabric and patterns. After one of the women took my measurements, I would tell the tailor what I wanted. Two days later, I could pick up the finished garment. I had to price bargain a little because it was expected, but at five dollars for something that was beautifully made, I tried to pay the full price.

In mid- winter which was July, and August, it gets all the way down to 60 degrees. Pretty cold with an ocean breeze blowing. I found that one of the problems with winter was all my pictures falling off the wall. In the summer when it is hot, I had put them all up with some blue stuff like silly putty, and they stayed up just fine. But in the winter, I have to put them up each morning. I don't mind too much because I like seeing all my family's faces.

During the two years I was there (1983–85), the Japanese were pouring money into Fiji. They bought a number of resorts and businesses. One of their bequests was an eight-and-one-half million-dollar nursing school for Fiji. I was against it because Fiji couldn't afford to maintain or equip the new building. Also the students would be trained on equipment they would never see again. However, in spite of many protests, the day came for the groundbreaking. There was a big celebration with the Japanese Ambassador, and Dr. Kurisangila, the Minister of Health and many other dignitaries present. The man who was the head of the company, which will do the construction, gave a long speech in Japanese. No one had a clue about what he was saying but it was great fun to watch the faces. Then the Fijians gave the traditional *savusavu* greeting complete with yaqona, chanting, and dancing. My students were beautifully dressed in tapa cloth and leaves with their faces painted. They danced, and it was good to see them enact this part of their culture. I was used to seeing them in their lavender uniforms or casual clothes.

My 60th Birthday

Seated Fijian dance-"meke"

CAROL PHILLIPS

Climbing coconut tree-Distributed by Caines Jannif Limited

Market- Suva

FIJI AND ME

police band

me washing clothes at sisters quarters NOTE SNARL

CAROL PHILLIPS

The Bottle Man

Hospital visiting hours

CHAPTER 17

The Beauty of Fiji

THE BEAUTY OF Fiji kept me fascinated. I'll try to describe what I saw and felt.. We were on the wet side of the island, which gave us rain almost every day. The day would dawn bright, clear, and sunny. Later the clouds would gather for artistic effect. Then there would come a few minutes of hard rain, followed by a misty rain. No one carried an umbrella because the warm tropical breeze soon had us dry. After that came the rainbows. They often happened at sunset and I kept looking from side to side. It's the best show in town.

There are a lot of palm trees, frangipani trees, and many bushes, with lovely brilliant flowers that smell wonderful. I think of my son, Charles, who liked my hibiscus. Here, the blossoms are six inches across and many are double. I often ate a guava picked from the bush outside the door. We had an avocado tree thirty-feet- high covered with avocados. The papaya trees. keep having new crops off-and-on all year.. We had many lemon trees. They make a wonderful tea here with lemon leaves. The richness and sumptuous quality of everything is a delight.

I have always loved the ocean and could see it through my windows in most of the places I lived. The coral reefs all around stop the breakers, and the colors of the water inside the reefs, and outside is vividly different—all shades of blue and green.

In the morning, the birds go crazy in a delightful way. There are so many different kinds and each sings its' own wonderful song. There are many large beautifully colored parrots and a number of tiny ones with red heads and tails, and green bodies. Mynah and bulbul birds walk in and out of the windows. There are few screens here. Mostly, windows are open all day and wooden shutters are let down at night.

coastline on Batiki Island

mulberry, frangipani and palm

CAROL PHILLIPS

papaya tree outside my door

coastline on Batiki Island

FIJI AND ME

CHAPTER 18

Hurricanes

WE HAD FOUR hurricanes while I was in Fiji. I have described "Hina" elsewhere because I rode her out on a ship. We had two in one week. During one, I was with Mona in the sister's quarters. We got prepared with drinking water and food, and were ready to tough it out. We got some strong winds and rain, but the storm veered a bit and hit the west side of Vita Levu badly. There were twenty seven deaths, mostly of people who did weird things like trying to swim to a downed tree to get coconuts or breadfruit. Someone was electrocuted hanging up clothes on a wire clothes line during the storm. A ship went down and those deaths were unavoidable. A friend from the US Embassy asked me over when the second one was expected. She went to bed and slept through the whole thing. But with the winds howling and trees crashing down around the house, I couldn't sleep. The electricity went off so I got a candle and a book, and read until about 4:00 AM when the winds abated a little. In the early morning, I heard the chain saws, and saw several men cleaning up. I felt that I had to get back to my house so I went carefully down to the road. A man was passing in a car and gave me a ride to the bus station. I took a bus out to where I lived and found chaos. One tree had fallen through the roof, and six or seven more were leaning against it. I had a difficult time getting in—climbing over tree trunks and debris. The inside of the house was all right except for drifts of leaves which had blown in through the louvers. I had closed everything up tightly, but it had been quite a wind. I believe this one was called "Gavin." There was no electricity for about six weeks. After that, winds were strange for several weeks, and no planes could land. It was amazing how well people managed with kerosene lamps and stoves. Everyone shared what they had to eat. Many of the fruit trees were stripped, so we did without fresh fruit for a while. I was so used to hurricanes by the time the fourth one came, that I hardly noticed. I was safe in the sister's quarters which had been standing securely for many years.

CHAPTER 19

End of Service Preparation

THERE WAS A lot to be done in the last weeks before leaving Fiji. I had to fill out a number of forms at the Peace Corps office. While I was there I asked my programmer if she would give me a recommendation for volunteering at the World Health Organization. She said, "No, I won't." You shouldn't be a volunteer anymore. You have too much to give." She told me that she had already sent a letter recommending me for a job at the Peace Corps office in DC when I return. She suggested that I write a follow- up letter to tell them I'd take it. I had heard about the position in DC. They wanted a mature person with a public health background, public speaking ability and some experience in the Peace Corps. It seemed that I met all the criteria, so I wrote that letter and sent it off on the next plane.

The Fijian Ministry of Health asked me if I would stay on and direct the family planning program. I said, "I believe that family planning would be better received coming from a local person, preferably a man. It should be someone who understands the peoples' thoughts and feelings from the inside." The woman who was trying to recruit me said, "But you do, kalokalo." That was one of the best compliments I could receive. . Family planning is a serious problem because the Fijians and Indians are each trying to have more babies so they will have more power. There are not enough resources or jobs to provide for this steadily increasing population. I was glad that the people at the Ministry had valued my work. I didn't consider it because I don't believe that a white person should be telling dark skinned people how to live their lives.

I looked through my clothes to see what to leave behind. It's hard for me to give clothes away because I never get anything I don't like. I got several boxes of things packed and left them in the area where the young staff nurses live. I left a note saying, "Take anything you like." When I got back they were all gone. I hope they enjoyed them as much as I did. We had a close of conference convocation back at the President Hotel that was interesting. It had a number of seminars about "Is there life after Fiji?" Many of the group left before the two-year contract had been completed. About thirty of us were there. We were glad to see one another again and trade stories. Several men wanted to extend because they had married Indian girls. Most of us had enjoyed our time in Fiji but were glad to be going home.

CHAPTER 20

My Last Day

IT'S NOVEMBER 30, my last morning in Fiji. I want to record this whole day so I can relive it. The birds are singing merrily. I never did find out what that bird was with the tiny body and the large transparent wings.

The Rucksack group gave me a great farewell party last night. Ted said that he wanted the first dance with me. He did some sort of boogie to the rock music. I finally got into his rhythm. I have loved getting to know Kim. We have so much in common even though she is Joan's age. I gave my turtle rock to Robert and he was pleased. It's sad to think that I won't see most of these people ever again. After the party, Kim and I decided we wanted to go down together to see the sunset for one last time. It went down into the water like a big beautiful ball of fire. She gave me my last hug in Fiji.

I've had an eventful day. I believe everything is packed because I couldn't get one more thing into the suitcase I bought here in Fiji. It may be shoddy, but it was big and inexpensive which was just what I wanted. I packed it yesterday, but Kitti didn't like the way I packed it so she repacked it. She did a much better job. When I started to zip it, the whole top pulled off. I got a needle and thread, and sewed it together, and then roped it shut in three places—the Fiji way. What is left, I'll put in my large tapa cloth purse as a carry-on. I'm looking at a beautiful bougainvillea which is a deep grape color. The beauty of Fiji has been a constant joy and inspiration.

I came across from Suva this morning in one of the most beautiful days I've ever seen and almost lost it on the bus. Many tears. Before I left Kitti and all the nursing sisters, we said our goodbyes, and were all crying. I'm in Nadi now at a hotel near the airport. At lunch, a young man named Andrew, asked to join me. He has just come to work here. I was glad to have someone to talk to because I was so miserable. He was interesting, and we talked about all sorts of things. He was eager to hear about Fiji. A beautiful black-and-yellow butterfly just landed on my arm to say goodbye.

I have changed my five US dollars into Fiji dollars because that is the fee paid to leave the airport. I have kept one of each of the Fiji monies to show my family because they are beautiful. I will leave the rest of my Fiji money with one of the maids at the airport.

The last few days have been wonderful because I've been savoring each person and each thing I see. I've even thought kindly of the hospital, and brushing mouse turds off my clothes so I could put them on. I never did figure out how mice can get into a closed drawer.

There is so much of me that will stay here in Fiji. Perhaps this is part of immortality, what we leave of ourselves to others. A lot of Fiji will come with me. There is so much about this place that I have loved.

My daughter, Liz, got it right when she said, "When you can get unconnected, come on back." True, but it's not easy because I think a lot of me will stay behind. Jumbled thinking a bit, but it's making some sort of sense at the moment. I'm deeply sad to leave Fiji and the life I have lived and loved here.

The airplane is such a sterile atmosphere with its own little world. Perhaps it is a good place to start the transition from one world to the other.

CHAPTER 21

Epilogue

DURING MY LIFE in Fiji, I tape recorded the things that were happening to me almost every day. I wanted to share this strange, wonderful life I was having with my children. They passed the tapes around and transcribed them. My daughter Nancy saved all my letters. I had a lot of material and they urged me to write it all into a book. My grandson, James, gave me a deadline. He was going on a two-year mission for his church. He said that he wanted to read the book when he returned. Sadly, he couldn't because I had been so busy doing other things that the book had been put on my back burner.

Now, twenty-five years later, I found that the time was right and I dug out the notes. I have had a joyful summer reliving my life in Fiji. Thinking and feeling about the people, places, and events has brought back so many happy and sad memories. I was surprised at my almost obsessive desire to get back to my notes so I could continue experiencing the feelings I was writing about. I was engrossed. I looked that up in the dictionary and it meant, "Caught up, consumed, taken up with." All of those words fitted. This has been a labor of love. I hope you have enjoyed reliving it with me.

AUTHOR BIOGRAPHY

CHICAGO WAS MY home town, but I grew up in Green Bay, Wisconsin. We loved those Packers. I went back to Chicago to study nursing. This was during WWII, when we all wanted to help in the war to end wars. What I had wanted to be was an English professor so I could read and write all the time. I found that nursing was a magic carpet in many ways.

I married a doctor from North Carolina. We moved to Southern Pines and I was glad to raise my six children in a place where the winter wasn't nine months long. My first vision of North Carolina was in April. Everything was in full bloom and I remember feeling that I had died and gone to heaven. People have said that it must have been difficult to have six children, but my memories are of enjoying it-- most of the time. My husband's midlife crisis ended our marriage. At forty five, I went back to college to finish a graduate degree. I began a career in nursing which included teaching. My writing during my nursing career had more to do with work sheets and constructing tests than fun. I did enjoy writing long letters to my children and grandchildren as they came along. In those days people wrote letters.

I have always loved to travel. When an opportunity came to circumnavigate the globe with a friend, I took it. We spent a wonderful month in Japan, Thailand, Nepal, India, Dubai, UK and Canada before returning. I remember well how grateful I was to be home in the US. I'd heard about people kissing the soil of their homeland and I understood.

I married a former Duke art professor who had decided to paint full time. He said he would find a place where a nurse and an artist could live happily. He found Key West. I rented my house, packed my car and started driving down the Keys. When I got there I found a houseboat named Miss Maggie and we lived on her. It was a real adventure for me. I worked in a mental health clinic and met some of the unusual people who inhabit Key West. A lot of stories were there to tell. After a year my story didn't include the artist.

I returned to North Carolina and went back to Duke Medical Center where I was head nurse of the Family Medicine Center. Residents were there learning to be family docs, something I admired. After three years, I found myself ready for a change. My children were all self- sufficient. I met a Peace Corps recruiter at a party and when I found I could go to Fiji I said, "Yes, please don't give that place to anyone else". It was a wonderful two years of my life. I loved the people and the beauty everywhere. I taught a bit and learned a lot.

One of the things I learned in Fiji was what they called "diridiri". It meant slow down and enjoy the moment. When I returned, I went back to Duke to work in psychiatry, but never full time. I arranged my work so I could take classes at the Duke school for older people, now called OLLI. I also facilitated classes on Reading Shakespeare and Great Books. I taught English as a second language at our library. Doing these things, slow and easy, gave me joy.

OLLI gave me more than a place to teach and learn. A classmate, Mal, and I shared a number of classes. Finally we decided to share life. Mal and I traveled to many places. He had been in the diplomatic service and knew Europe well, so I got to see some special places off the beaten path. He left for heaven on a train in Budapest after saying that our three week river cruise had been the happiest time of his life

Now, I live in a wonderful village called the Forest. I enjoy reading, writing, a bit of bridge, friends and family. This family now includes my four wonderful children, ten grandchildren with spouses, and twenty great grandchildren. Life is good

This book couldn't have been completed without the help of daughter, Janet and granddaughters, Anna and Margaret. Love and thanks.

CAROL PHILLIPS

Made in the USA
Middletown, DE
29 June 2024

56566156R00071